Sis, Is It You?

Discovering Self-Revelation

Tiffynee Terry-Thomas

RACQ SYMPHONY PUBLISHING
WWW.RACQSYMPHONY.COM

Note from the Author

I have tried to recreate events, locales and conversations from my memories of them. In order to maintain their anonymity in some instances, I may have changed some identifying characteristics and details such as physical properties, occupations, and places of residence.

Scriptures used throughout the book are taken from the King James Version unless otherwise noted.

© 2021 Sis, Is It You? Discovering Self-Revelation Vol 1

Cover design: Panagiotis Lampridis
Cover Photo: Angela Land Photography
Videographer: JD Hawthorne
Photographer: Ashley Birk

All rights reserved. No part of this book may be reproduced, scanned, or distributed in any printed or electronic form without the written permission of the publisher.

First Edition: 2021

Printed in the United States of America

ISBN-13: 978-0-998662-75-6

TABLE OF CONTENTS

Dedication

I would not know anything about self-revelation if it weren't for three essential people in my life, my husband Brandon, my oldest daughter Jai (identical twin), and my youngest daughter Jordyn (*Grandma* as we like to call her).

To Grandma, thank you for always serving it up to your momma, real deal Holyfield. Your ability to remind me at all times of what I'm destined to be has given me the ammunition to knock this book out. Thank you!

To my twin, God knew exactly what he was doing when He gifted me with you. You have taught me so much about little Tiffynee that I didn't realize I needed to know. You have been a fantastic teacher and student through this journey. I can't thank you enough for all that you have allowed me to be in your life. Shout out to my best friend!

To the love of my life and my soul mate. God gave you the patience and grace to provide me with room to grow into who I was destined to be. You allow me to be me, but you require only the best version of myself. You have always been my rock. Thank you for never leaving my side and always encouraging me to go hard or to go home!

FOREWORD

I remember the first time I laid eyes on Tiffynee Terry-Thomas. It was her sexologist certification video on Instagram and I instantly knew there was something special and genuine about this woman and I had to reach out. She was very pleasant, open and willing to help without any reservation at all.

We have both gone ahead to do things together and what stood out and continues to stand out for me is her raw hunger for God and to help strengthen and build healthy relationships and marriages.

In this book, you'll feel her authentic message, you'll feel like you're talking to, and listening to a big sister who's genuinely there to hold you by the hand and show you what is possible for YOU!

She has not only poured herself out in this masterpiece, but has also provided you with relatable, practical tools to help you rediscover you, become more intentional, more humble and have the courage to do and be who you are supposed to be.

What takes the cake for me is how she helps you relate better to "A Cool God".

As a certified relationship and marriage counselor, I HIGHLY RECOMMEND this book to you, and to everyone in your life because if we all knew better, we all will do better. Queen Tiffynee (as I fondly call her) has done an incredible job with this book and I am so proud of her and I am confident in the transformation that you are about to encounter.

Cecilia May Agu
Relationship, Marriage & Sex Coach
Bedroom Matters Int'l

Prologue

I t's been a long time coming, but momma, I finally made it.

This book is just the beginning of a journey that I've traveled once before and one that I pray you will accompany me on again. *Sis, Is it you realizing the toxic in you* was going to be my first book because it was my initial problem. There are and were many toxic things that made themselves right at home within myself. My goal was to rid myself of as many deadly toxins that I could to preserve my life and my purpose. Toxic things like our bad attitudes, uncontrolled mouths, inability to hold ourselves accountable, and so much more. Sis, it was me, and I said to myself, *"Now I know if I'm walking around here leaving toxic turds everywhere, I'm sure I have been stepping in other peoples' ish as well."*

Growing up, I had one parent who didn't cuss, drink, do drugs, or barely raise their voice: my father. My mother was a cursing Christian (let her tell it, I'm lying, lol). Although that was probably the worst thing I saw her do growing up, the realization of how things are easy to plant into your children became quite apparent, while raising my kids. I realized now that I still cuss to this day because it's a bad habit that I'm trying to ween myself off of. Throughout my self-discovery, I have attempted to participate in fasting's that could help me refrain from cussing.

It was day 3 of my 21 day fast of no cussing. I texted my good Pastor friend and I said, *"I realized what the problem is for my cussing."* Of course, he inquired. I responded and said, *"It's my environment. Do you think that you can take my kids and husband for the next three weeks so that I can get through this?"* We both laughed. I think we both knew that this fast was just the beginning of my detox, and it was going to take some time to deliver me from this.

I may slip up a few times throughout this book, but what I'm trying to display is the realness of who I am at the core. The truth is sometimes I cuss, but I love Jesus with my whole heart, so don't judge me, LOL. The truth is that we all have flaws, but the things that we can change, we really should work hard at doing so. Cussing doesn't define me. I leave you with one takeaway that I have learned about this cussing thing: it defeats the purpose of you using the word if you don't know what the word means.

Fuck– means to damage- I used to say FTK (Fuck These Kids) truthfully because they consistently got on my doggone nerves. When GOD placed it on my heart to look at the words I was using, it gave me perspective, which allowed me to curve my appetite for unnecessary cussing. Simmer on that for a sec!

This book is all about the tools you will need before going through a detox. As seen on TV, detoxing is not for the weak. I acquired these tools throughout my journey and placed them within this book to make you strong and build you up for this journey. I'm a survivor of this discovery, so I know you will do fine, but please be advised I'm definitely coming for you!

Sis, It's you!

INTRODUCTION

Welcome! So, what brings you to this book of discovery?

My guess is that you picked up this book because you need a revelation. Whatever the reason is, I welcome you with open arms and a warm heart. I know that this isn't easy, and it takes some real essential qualities to get you this far. So, I will say, "YOU MADE IT!!!"

Let me first welcome you to a place where peace resides permanently. Storms do come through here from time to time. If you adapt to the few mandatory characteristics, you will make it through every one of them. I am happy to see that you arrived safely. I am Tiffynee. I am your guide, and I am here to show you around. Enjoy your exploration. You are in for a ride. I am proud to see you here!

Are you just visiting or moving here permanently? No need to answer that right now. You have three books to decide that. It's time to shift the atmosphere in your life.

> *It's Me, not you*
> *It's not you, it's me,*
> *The reason for my rise*
> *And the blame for my fall.*
> *The efforts behind my success*
> *And the lack thereof in case of*
> *Failure.*
> *It's not you; it's me.*

-Sonali Kolge

Raise your hand (only in your head so you don't feel silly) if you've ever used the phrase above. Research says that this is one of the main excuses used during a relationship breakup. Whether it be romantic or platonic, this is the reason given. When people use the phrase above, they aren't associating themselves with the blame, they use themselves as scapegoats to avoid the admission of ones' toxic traits. So, what exactly *is* a scape goat? Well, I'm glad you asked.

Scape Goat- Someone or something that is assigned the blame or made to take the fall for something they didn't do.

This admission is a temporary escape from dealing with yourself because, typically, the other person is challenging you to be something you are not prepared to be. Accepting that you are the problem takes a long time to come to grips with for many people. It's ok. I'm here for you.

I struggled with this for quite some time, and I have gone on many self-discoveries. I've always enjoyed the essence of my experiences throughout my life, and sometimes I would unknowingly overindulge in those experiences. For example, I grew up debating everything anyone said. If it didn't make sense to me, I would create arguments just for me to get someone to see my side of things. That behavior was not healthy. It became a toxic trait that I overused so that I would win the argument. After many failed self-discoveries about this recurring issue, I needed to understand why I had become so thirsty for that type of attention and why the only thing that was appetizing to my ego was the need to be correct. It didn't make me a victor in any of the situations. It made me the victim, and that drained me. It was feeding my spirit snacks and, we all know that snacks aren't fulfilling. They are just tasty for the time being. By the time I realized this, I had manifested an addiction. Along with other toxic behaviors, they would all end up teaching me precious lessons that would one day enhance my life's quality.

What snacks are you using to supplement hearty meals?

Do you happen to know what feeds your spirit? I do. It's called purpose. We will get into that later.

My Journey

During each discovery, I uncovered that all my ups and downs had a tremendous purpose. I just needed the right set of tools to get me through. I have succumbed to many judgments and unsolicited opinions about my life, but I made it my point to honor the tools given to me so I wouldn't become distracted by outside noise.

We all make mistakes. We will watch other people make the same or similar mistakes and make all kinds of judgments and statements about what we would have done better. Yet, how often do we take the time to take a step back and say, "What is it about my mistakes that are causing issues in my life?"

One of the hardest things we struggle with within ourselves is genuine self-reflection (360). It's easy for us to point the finger and call the kettle black yet be oblivious to own our mess-ups.

Why do the majority of us fail to learn from our constant mistakes?

SIS, IT IS YOU!
IT IS ME!
IT IS US!

It is time for us to look within and examine ourselves with fresh eyes and open ears. We have to remove the filter from our eyes so we can see clearly and remove the muffle that blocks us from hearing what we don't want to hear. So, as a Black Beautiful Strong Woman, I say this with all sincerity. Get your backpack and let's go!

Word Wheel

Use this wheel when you start to feel anything that you can't describe; look the word up to help you better understand it. The word wheel allows you to steer clear of the cliche emotions and will enable you to identify with how you genuinely feel.

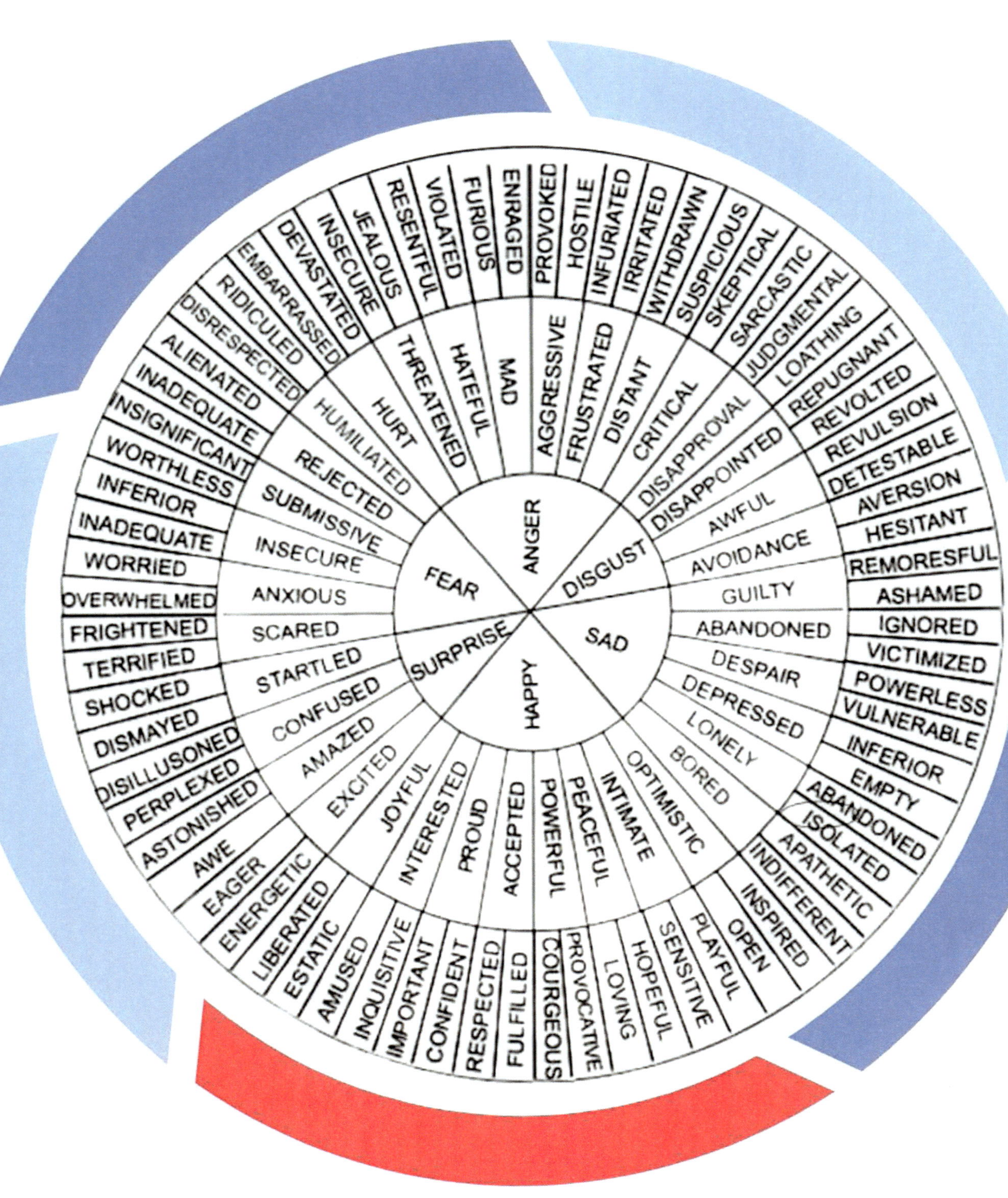

Chapter 1

Discovering Self Revelation

Look into the pool of water. Lies disappear because the water is clear, and the truth reveals itself by reflecting in the transparent water. Discover Self-Revelation – Tiffynee

I believe that most people see the word **REVELATION** and genuinely have no idea what it means. I say that because this word only stood out to me because it was the last chapter in the Bible. My interpretation of the word, when comparing to the Book of Revelations in the Bible, is God finally revealing Himself. Throughout the Bible, He allows stories to be told about His presence, authenticity, thoughts, abilities, and promises. To me, it's like God is standing in the mirror and allowing Himself to call out all that He sees in His reflection. Those who get scared from reading the Book of Revelations or hear horror stories about it have allowed themselves to forget that uncovering ones true self will reveal the good, bad, and ugly, but once that happens you are able to live a fulfilled life.

People attach definitions of words to memories, moments, and feelings instead of applying the correct meaning to the word. This is because the experiences and obstacles we have been through are so powerful we can't avoid them. It's easy to dismantle opportunities for ourselves just because we might lack the proper knowledge to move forward in life. In order to create growth for ourselves we must divorce this habit and slow down enough to re-learn things so we can have a better understanding of what's going on around us. Here is the definition of the word, revelation.

Revelation - A surprising and previously unknown fact, especially one that is made known in a dramatic way.

When I discovered my biggest revelation, I admit I was pleasantly surprised, appalled and in denial. SIS, I WAS TOXIC! And in more ways than one. Once this discovery was made, it wasn't easy to turn off. Let's compare this to an example. When you buy a car and, all of a sudden, you start seeing that car everywhere. Once something is discovered it can never be undiscovered again. Discovering Self-Revelation can be the start of a new life for you. I am determined to allow every year to be a year of growth and development for my family and myself. I'm aware that getting to this point can and will be challenging for some, so I wrote this book to give you the tools and instructions you will need before taking you into the wilderness, unprepared, to fully discover yourself.

How well do you know the person who lives inside your body? Let me take a wild guess your answer is, "Pretty well who doesn't know themselves, right?"

Wrong. Studies show that most people are reluctant to self-discovery, fearing that they might not like what they discover. Let's all agree that we all fall short of our best selves at times. The goal is to be *like* Jesus, not identical *to* Jesus. This means we are not perfect, and I believe that's why God created grace. I have great news! Because of God's grace, our lives can be changed. So, what exactly is grace?

Grace - is unmerited mercy.

Now, what is mercy?

Mercy - compassion or forgiveness shown toward someone whom it is within one's power to punish or harm.

There Is Always a Correct Way

cor·rect
adjective

- free from error: in accordance with fact or truth.

I'm not here to tell you in detail how you can correct anything in your life, I'm just here to represent the word *correct* and encourage you to become open to loving the word. When I use to see the word *correct* or I would hear the word *correct,* I would immediately think that someone was trying to tell me I was wrong and by wrong, I mean stupid. Can we normalize that you are not stupid just because you are wrong about something? There is a high possibility that you really didn't have a better answer or the correct answer?

This topic arose on a day I was talking to my oldest daughter. Right now, she is a hormonal teenager with a heart of gold and a mouth full of spitfire. SEND HELP NOW! SOS! During this abrupt conversation she and I were having, she spouted out, "Oh here you go again...always wanting to be right and making someone feel stupid."

In an absent-minded parenting moment, I normally would have lost my marbles, but I had prepared myself for this conversation.

Preparation is always necessary to succeed in your mission.

My response to her was that I didn't have the ability to make her feel any type of way, but I wasn't going to take away from what she was experiencing. I explained to her that the reason she might be feeling that way is because she created the assumption in her head that when she doesn't know something, she feels stupid and in return she will project those feelings on to me as if I feel that way about her too. I asked her had she ever thought to just asked me what my intent was? Her answer was no!

I did something that most people and most parents especially (black parents) feel uncomfortable doing. *Gasps*

I explained myself to her. Yes, I know. You're shocked...especially if you would have heard her tone.

I told my daughter that when she doesn't know something, that is a perfect moment for me to educate them. If someone can explain to me that they knew exactly what they were supposed to do, but then did the opposite, I will pull out a card from the category of stupid and place it on the table as an option to place them in. On many occasions, that wasn't the case for her. I'm the parent and I'm supposed to be teaching her about life. Most of the time when we don't feel good about something we have done, it's often because deep down inside we know there was a better way to do it.

People tend to view themselves in the most positive ways instead of the most honest ways. While things outside of us also contribute to our success or failures, what counts is what's on the inside. Managing your thoughts, emotions, motives, and self-talk will allow great rewards during this self-discovery journey. You have to be ok with not knowing everything.

In Episode 1, Season Four of *Insecure*, Molly turns to Issa and says, *"You know your life doesn't have to be this messy, right? Sometimes I think that you like that shit!"*

I love Molly's concept, but not necessarily in that particular situation. Still, I'm convinced that some of us prefer to stay in complicated and messy situations. Do you know how often I ask people if they like to be mad? OFTEN! When I ask them, they look at me with a stunned face, like *"I cannot believe you think I want to be angry all the time."* NEWS FLASH! Being mad is a CHOICE. Sis, if you are mad all the time, you have become comfortable with being mad. Anything that keeps recurring in your life, good or bad, you like it.

It is quite common for people to stay in their natural environments. Researchers say that humans can adapt to almost anything. I just wished more of us adapted to true happiness and success.

The idea that most humans don't learn from their own mistakes have a better chance of learning from their successes than their own mistakes has been bounced around for quite some time. Let's take it a step further. A study at MIT showed that the brain demonstrated that it retains more after a success than past failures. The brain neurons can keep a memory of recent successes and failures during learning and perform better after doing it right than after doing it wrong. The research indicates that what society suspects are that people learn from their own mistakes, which isn't true.

> *"We have shown that brain cells keep track of whether recent behaviors were successful or not," Miller said. Furthermore, cells became more finely tuned to what the animal was learning when the behavior was successful. After a failure, there was little or no change in the brain — nor was there any improvement in behavior. (Oppong, n.d.)*

Furthermore, researchers found that if you repeated the same mistakes, you would have a less active brain. Yes, I said it. If you are sitting here at this very moment, wondering if your brain activity registers on the low side, I guess that would be determined by inhow many times it takes you to get it. There are ways to unlearn this behavior and head towards a life that consists of more wins! All it takes is accepting that the issue isn't someone else, but yourself. SIS, IT'S YOU!

> *"A wise person learns from one's mistake, and a wiser one learns from other's mistakes, but the wisest person learns from another's successes."*
>
> *- Source, a whole bunch of people on Google. But John Maxwell said this one.*

I know individuals that think after surviving through being angry, mad, sad, etc. for so long. Why would they want to adapt to the UNKNOWN feeling of peace and or happiness? Like, who wants that? SIS, I WANT IT! From your social media feed, it looks like you think you want it too. Obtaining it is possible. It's not out of the ordinary. The one thing about the unknown is that it's foreign. So, what does foreign mean? It means strange and unfamiliar, so, adjust to it, but don't run from it.

DON'T BE SCARED
Self-Reflection is the Key

If you want to discover your best self, you must be transparent. This will require you to be honest about who you really are. It would help if you demanded honesty about yourself from yourself. The easiest person in the world to deceive is yourself, so avoid self-deception.

Self-deception is the action or practice of allowing oneself to believe that a false or unvalidated feeling, idea, or situation is true.

The scale is one of our biggest enemies to this date. I say this because no matter how often you avoid it or cling to it, it will let you down 90% of the time. I'm sure anyone male or female can attest to this because what you think in your mind versus what the scale registers will always differ. How? Self-Deception! Most of us will believe that whatever we are doing should or should not contribute to the scale. For example, let's say all of 2020 I sat in the house and ate junk the majority of the time. I get on the scale. It's 10lbs heavier than when I last got on it. I head over to my closet, pull out my favorite jeans, and attempt to squeeeeeze into them. To my surprise, I can't zip them up. I'm pissed because I'm trying to figure out when this happened and where the heck was I while it was happening.

SIS, YOU WERE RIGHT HERE! You were right there the entire time.

My mom experienced this recently. She constantly told me that she was refraining from greasy foods and watching what she ate. What I saw with my own eyes was her swinging by the burger joints and other fast-food places, grabbing something, but substituting things with a healthier option (sweet potato fries instead of regular fries). Her actions caused her to think that she was doing something great for her body. A few times, my daughter and I would call her out. She would deflect, deny and disagree with everything we said. Then she met up with the scale at the doctor's office. What they said to her was different than what she had been telling herself for the past few months. She finally had a moment where she was like, *"I have to stop doing this shit."* Yup, she cussed, lol. I laughed, but I knew that her days of deceiving herself about her weight were coming to an end. YALL the scale don't LIE.

It's easy to tell yourself all these wonderful things about yourself. Whatever you tell yourself, you will believe. One of the best ways to get to know yourself is to focus on your behaviors rather than your words. Let's think about this for a moment. If I'm always saying I'm nice or kind, people close to me tell me I'm mean and rude. My behaviors are not matching my thoughts and ideas of myself. I encountered this with the infamous Jordyn, my youngest daughter. I told her to be kind to her sister because being mean isn't nice. Jordyn hit me with, *"why don't you do the same?"* Yall, she was right. If I'm trying to teach my children something, but I can't model it myself, who am I to correct anyone?

Would you want your son or daughter to be with someone that exhibits the worst parts of you?

Simmer on that.

Self Deception

It's easy to tell yourself all these wonderful things about yourself, and whatever you tell yourself you will believe.

What have you been allowing yourself to believe about yourself that you want to acknowledge?
Write Down Below

One night, my husband and I got into an argument about whose turn it was to cook dinner (pre-weekly schedule that was created). Since I was the majority stakeholder in the kitchen during this time, my temporary and unstable emotions took over during the argument. I felt the debate had no just cause. I thought and assumed that I was the judge, jury, and executioner (in my household), I decided, it was case closed!

My thought process on that was if I have to cook, no one will eat!

See what I did right there? I just painted a picture for you to see, and I made myself the judge.

I hopped on the **Seek Validation Scene** (Instagram, Facebook, and Snapchat), and I begin to peruse as I usually do. but this day was a bit different. You see, as I was perusing social media, I saw a quote that said, *"You don't know what you got until it's gone."*

Me: You damn right. He will starve!

Seek Validation Scene: A cute picture, some random social media ad—boom, another sign.

Seek Validation Scene: Sponsored: Pisces horoscope. Jupiter is nearing the scene, and today will be the day of new beginnings and setting firm boundaries.

That post confirmed I shouldn't cook, and I should let them starve. That will teach them!! I need to be appreciated in this house, so I reposted it on my page.

If I only choose to see things my way, it leaves me looking at everything through my lens, which can be a limited lens depending on outside influences. My perspective kept me locked in a place of bitterness and self-righteousness. Perhaps some of you reading this might have felt sympathy for my husband and children. Most may even suggest that I should have softened my spirit and feed my lovely family. (P. S. You're right) There is always a better way to handle things like this. Drum roll, please! Social media does not have all the answers to all of life's challenges. Quite possibly, none of what I was seeing were signs at all. It was the Law of Attraction. You see, my energy can attract things that make me feel validated at the moment based on how I'm feeling. Also, it's who and what you follow. If you follow pages that limit your ability to think outside the norm versus following pages that allow you to learn and deposit good things in, you can determine your thought process.

It's easy to find yourself in a situation like this. You have the right to feel wronged or disadvantaged because of your title (Wife, Fiancé, Mom, sister, friend, and even all the men roles). My purpose in pointing this out to you is to show you that just because you feel like this doesn't mean that it is accurate or worth it. Sis, is it worth it to be mad about this? Can you figure out how not to be in a situation like this again?

Cognitive dissonance -the state of having inconsistent thoughts, beliefs, or attitudes, especially relating to behavioral decisions and attitude change.

Becoming fully aware and being accountable for your choices is key to living a healthier mental lifestyle. Give yourself permission to recognize and accept that we all suffer from cognitive dissonance at times.

Sis, me choosing not to feed my family didn't benefit anyone, including me. It's rare that one can go to bed with the guilt of knowingly hurting someone and not trying to fix it. If you don't experience that, read this book twice!

You are the Key

I have a good friend that frequently reminiscences about himself playing basketball in the 1980s. He never made it to the league. To this day, he faults his parents for him not being who he had dreamed of becoming. On numerous occasions, I wanted to ask his parents were they playing on the team as well, but I guess I would've just been a jack ass. Unfortunately, he doesn't take any accountability for his missed opportunity. He still allows himself to visit that place of disappointment quite frequently and he has been stuck in time literally and figuratively. Let's just say his closet is decked with fresh 90's gear as well. When people fail to reach their goals, they quickly begin playing the blame game. We find the person standing near the failed plan, which in this example represents his parents, coaches, and teammates. For you, it can mean anyone that isn't you. We attach the blame to them and then we look for the nearest exit and disappear.

This means that none of what happened is connected to us. We can only see others at fault for why we missed out on the opportunity. Many Christians, I know, blame the devil for anything that goes wrong in their life. From what I know, the devil cannot be with you all day, lol. So, the Enemy might be IN ME (meaning you). Most of the time, we are our own worst enemies. You are the key that unlocks a brighter future. Don't lose your key or give it away.

Mirror, Mirror Here I Am

Everyone has a mirror and when we look at them, some of us look radiant and positive, and some are dull and negative. For most people, they are oblivious of what they are until it gets addressed.

I know many people, including myself, who assumed their reflection was shining bright like a diamond, but that's nothing but a filter. Remove the filter so that you will be able to start this discovery. How many of us don't even feel pretty without using a snap chat filter? Sweetie, I get it. It makes me feel pretty as well, but when I go live, you're getting the real me. I need to become accustomed to the real me, not the filtered me. Everyday life is a challenge, and we as people will have to wrestle with daily struggles. Whether you like it or not, we must overcome these challenges, whether external or internal. We can't allow them to sabotage our lives. This process of self-discovery will be one of the most rewarding experiences you will ever encounter. It will not be easy, but you will get to tap into who you are and what God has in store for you. After reading through this entire book series, you will feel empowered to take on the world. As we start to strip you down to your core, you will get to take away layers of yourself that are not who you are. There will be times that you will need to step away from this discovery to regain your composure because what you may discover could get intense. I will not act like this process is easy. During my journey, I have shed many tears and let go of a lot of people. I will add this disclaimer: if you do the work and find out who you are, it will change your entire life for the better.

The Filter in Your Life can Distort the Reality of Yourself!

When was the last time you took a picture without using a filter to make yourself look better?

When was the last time you posted a real clear picture of who you are?

When was the last time that you stood in the mirror and called yourself out?

I had to ask myself these questions quite frequently during my self-revelation journey. It became apparent to me that I had become comfortable with what the filter covered up. I had completely ignored what was underneath because, to me, it wasn't worth fixing if I was the only one who could see it. I had mastered the ability to ignore a problem that had a better solution to it.

> *"Before I ask you to sit with me,*
> *I must be able to sit with myself,*
> *Before I ask you to accept the Pain myself,*
> *Before I ask you to love me,*
> *I have to be madly in love with myself."*

> *-C. Thoth*

Mirror, Mirror

It's time to remove the filter.

Write down what you see in yourself at this moment.

Focus on the things you have control over. In most cases, you have no control over what has happened to you. You are not your emotions or your thoughts. You can only decide that you won't allow them to define who you are. One of the healthiest things you can do is accept that it is a part of your life's journey but refuse to let it take you off course. True freedom comes from forgiveness, and I can honestly attest to that. It's my choice to forgive. Forgiveness gives me my power back over the situation. The amount of strength that I gain and the ability to have a new perspective is worth more than harboring anything that doesn't belong to me.

I have experienced some of the most treacherous betrayals, and it has come from everyone, including myself. During those moments, there was a lot of anger and resentment that tried to reside in my heart. Sis, they had unpacked and made themselves right at home. I had a close friend hurt me recently. During this time in my life, I couldn't understand why this was happening to me. I wanted to be angry, sad, hurt, and shocked, but I kept hearing this voice saying, *"Do you think they know what they are doing?"* I had to take a step back and agree. The voice was the Big Homie, but it was clear, and it felt authentic. At that moment, I didn't try to negotiate with my feelings, I just took God's word and issued out my forgiveness. I had to remind myself that the person I was dealing with wasn't a slight bit stupid, but did they have the ability to allow their emotions and feelings to supersede the truth. This behavior wasn't anything new to me. So, with all the love in my heart, I forgave them and moved on. Moving on doesn't mean that we are all hunky-dory. I know that they had no control over that, and I had control over my anger and my forgiveness. You see, I don't like being mad at all, and I honestly don't think anyone is worth it to be that mad at, especially when you know they didn't know any better. Sis, don't let them take you off course. Politely let them off at the next rest stop. If it is meant to be, they will catch up with you, hopefully.

Harboring unforgiveness is like taking a drink of poison and hoping it will kill someone else

- Anonymous

Self-realization doesn't happen overnight. It will take time and practice. If you use these tools habitually, in these next seven chapters, it will become a habit. Once you finally feel like you are in more control over your life, you are ready to level up. Throughout these chapters, you will have worksheets to coincide with each chapter. The goal is to help you work through this slowly, so it sticks. I filled this book with the tools, gems, and keys you will need to accompany you on this long journey of detoxing. Learning how each tool works and applying them correctly to this discovery will allow you to be as successful as I was.

Before we dive in, I want to give you one more helpful reference to refer back to while reading through this series.

VOCABULARY

Don't worry, I felt the same way when I typed it out. Man! This is like school, only this time I need you to receive all this goodness and apply it to your daily life moving forward. The following words you will see quite often throughout this series. You will need to know what this means to use it correctly to your life.

1. **Discernment**- The ability to judge well.
   a. Deliberate practice for taking on discernment is necessary.
   b. Practice entering a conversation with God about the little things in your life.
   c. Practice learning to listen – He may not speak to you as He speaks to others.
   d. Don't expect to be able to hear if you've never listened before. You must be still and concentrated to listen to him. It would help if you were quiet, shutdown your outside thoughts, and focus on hearing him.
   e. The difference between wisdom and discernment is that wisdom is a deep understanding of a subject, and discernment is the activity of determining the value and quality of a specific topic.
2. **Integrity**- The quality of being honest and having strong moral principles, a moral uprightness.
   a. Having integrity means that you live according to your deepest values. You're honest with everyone, and you always keep your word. Integrity is a highly valued trait, especially in leaders.
   b. Being dependable and following through on commitments.
   c. Being open and honest when communicating with others.
   d. Holding yourself accountable and owning up to your shortcomings.
3. **Mindfulness**- A mental state achieved by focusing one's awareness on the present moment.
   a. Calmly acknowledging and accepting one's feelings, thoughts, and bodily sensations, used as a therapeutic technique.
   b. Intention –from practicing **mindfulness, your purpose is what you hope to get**.
   c. Attention –your inner or outer **mindfulness** experiences is about paying attention (to. ...).
   d. Attitude – paying attention to **mindfulness** individual perspectives such as curiosity, acceptance, and kindness.

4. **Humility**- Freedom from pride or arrogance. The quality or state of being humble is to accept the honor of what's morality

5. **Grace**- - is unmerited mercy.

6. **Mercy**- compassion or forgiveness shown toward someone whom it is within one's power to punish or harm.

Discovery Tools Needed

I have listed below the items that we will collect throughout this book. Don't be in a rush to get all of these in one read, and they will take time to develop. Don't let your ego and pride check all these boxes prematurely. Have integrity and humility while doing this simple activity.

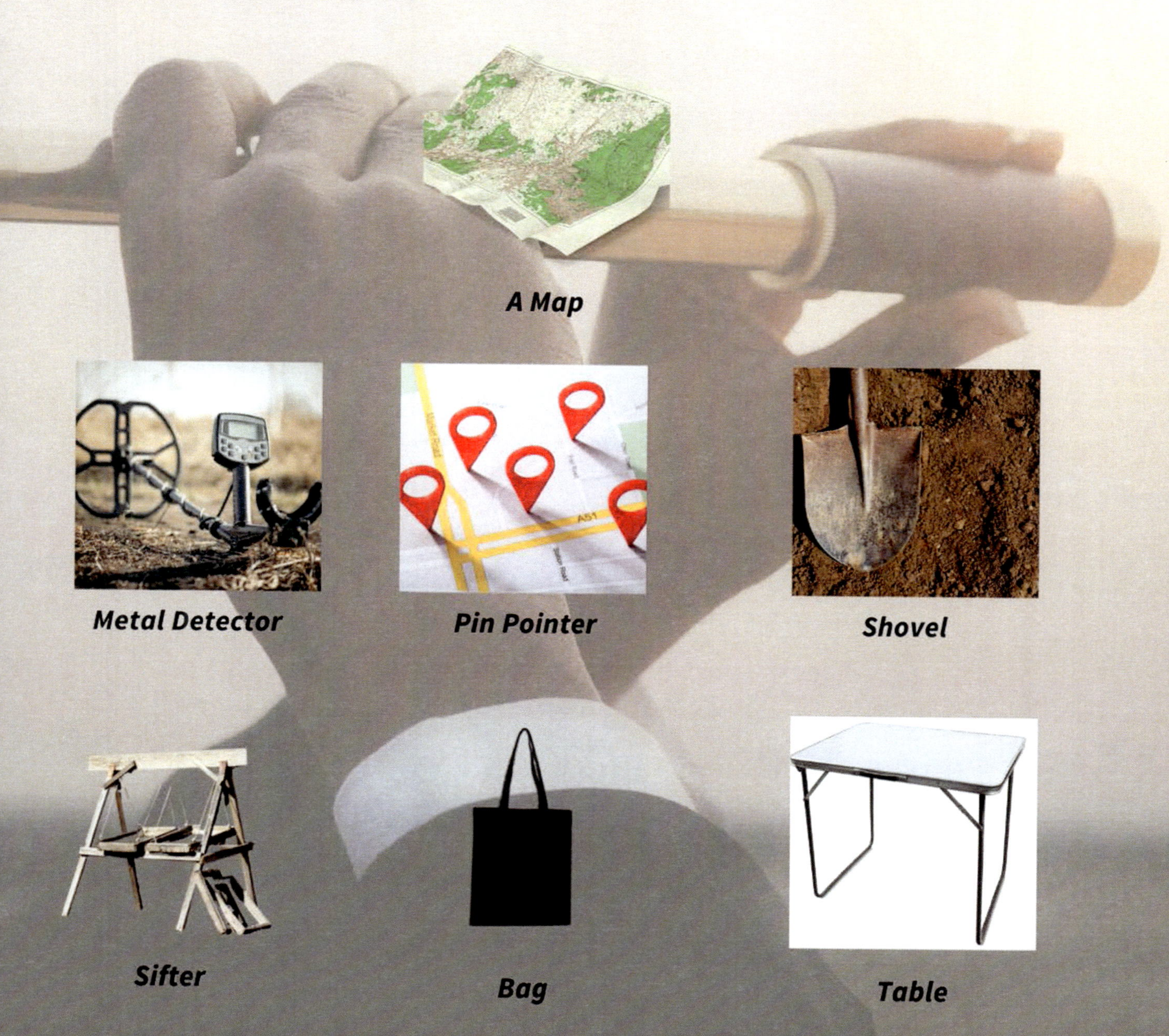

A Map

Metal Detector

Pin Pointer

Shovel

Sifter

Bag

Table

GOD'S PROMISE

Self Revelation

Examine yourselves to see whether you are in your faith. Test yourselves. Do you not realize this about yourselves, that Jesus Christ is in you?—unless indeed you fail to meet the test! I hope you will find out that we have not forgotten the test. (We pray to God that you may not do wrong—not that we may appear to have met the test. That you may do what is right even though we may seem to have failed.) For we cannot do anything against the truth, but only for the truth. For we are glad when we are weak, and you are strong. Your restoration is what we pray for. For this reason I write these things while I am away from you, that when I come I may not have to be (severe) in my use of the authority that the Lord has given me for building up and not for tearing down

2nd Corinthians 13:5-10 Esv

Talk to God

This is one of the easiest things to do because it's just like journaling but with a purpose and person in mind.

THE TIFFANATOR

Chapter 2

Map - Get Directions

Maps are an important part of our everyday lives.

We use them for driving directions, to look up restaurants or activities. We can even use smartphone maps to locate different types of things. The map that I will be gifting you this chapter is going to allow you to locate the specific area where your heart is currently at.

"Everyone thinks of changing the world, but no one thinks of changing themselves."

– Leo Tolstoy

How important do you think it should be to map out your heart's placement before starting this discovery? For me, it was imperative to take some time out to figure out where my heart was and then decide where I needed it to be. To complete this task, I was going to need some clear direction. One of the coolest things about the Bible is that the stories are so relatable. It references so many things about the placement of your heart. It makes me wonder, how can anyone deny that this isn't from the Big Homie up above? Who is concerned about the posture of your heart? Please name someone besides me and maybe your parents.

The one most significant thing to have is a sense of direction. If you are starting this journey and have no idea where to start, this chapter should give you a good idea of where to begin.

di·rec·tion

noun

1. a course along which someone or something moves.
2. the management or guidance of someone or something.

Where are You Going and Where Have You Been?

Most of us can tell you where we have been, but very few people I have encountered can tell you where they are headed. It's hard to know where you are going if you lack direction in your life.

Let's talk about where we have been. It could simply be that we have been at home. After all, we are in a Pandemic. But, where has your heart been? The best way I can describe the state of what my heart used to be in is like a phone who's owner refuses to put it in a case because it's too bulky. The phone is cracked from corner to corner. Can I say that most phone users don't care as much for their phones as they think they do lol? That's how the majority of us taking care of our hearts. My heart had been all sorts of cracked and screwed over, with no protective case in sight. I tend to think that people refuse to see the case for their phone because it doesn't look aesthetically pleasing. Most people apply that same level of thinking when it comes to guarding their hearts. It isn't attractive to society to have boundaries, standards, or live by direct principles created to make life great.

Consider your heart to be planted in soil. *Soil is a natural resource used for the growth of land and plants.* The soil that I'm referring to is around your heart. What things are you allowing your soil to inherit and soak up?

Heart Build Up

Did you know that there's things that can block your heart from getting the blood supply it needs? Things that you allow to reside in your heart as well can block it from getting the nutrients it needs.
Below write around the perimeter of the heart things you have allowed to build up in your heart.

Arriving somewhere unfamiliar can make you extremely uncomfortable. I'm sure where your heart is currently is somewhere you've been before. When you leave your heart unattended for some time, I can imagine how many thorn bushes and weeds have invaded your precious soil. I'm sure many of us have driven by abandoned houses that are covered by untamed wilderness and we sit back and think, *"Who would allow all this to happen?"* Sis, it was me.

My hearts' soil was untamed, and to be honest, who knows what was growing in my soil. I know that I had not been tending to it as I should have. My heart was solid like a rock. What I mean by that is I really had a hard time feeling things. I had allowed so much hurt and anger to reside in my heart that it had turned to stone. It was even hard to care about things when it came to my kids, let alone my husband. That ship had left the dock and returned so many times because it was comfortable. My life was hard, and I was just living with no purpose and no feelings. My heart had suffered so much that I felt the only way to protect it was to freeze it. Hell, most things you freeze have an extended expiration date. Little did I know that frozen anger and hurt only leaves you with the task of unthawing it and eating it regardless. I didn't like where I was at and I didn't like how I felt, but it was me that allowed my soil to become untamed and allowed my heart to become hard.

Heart Check Up

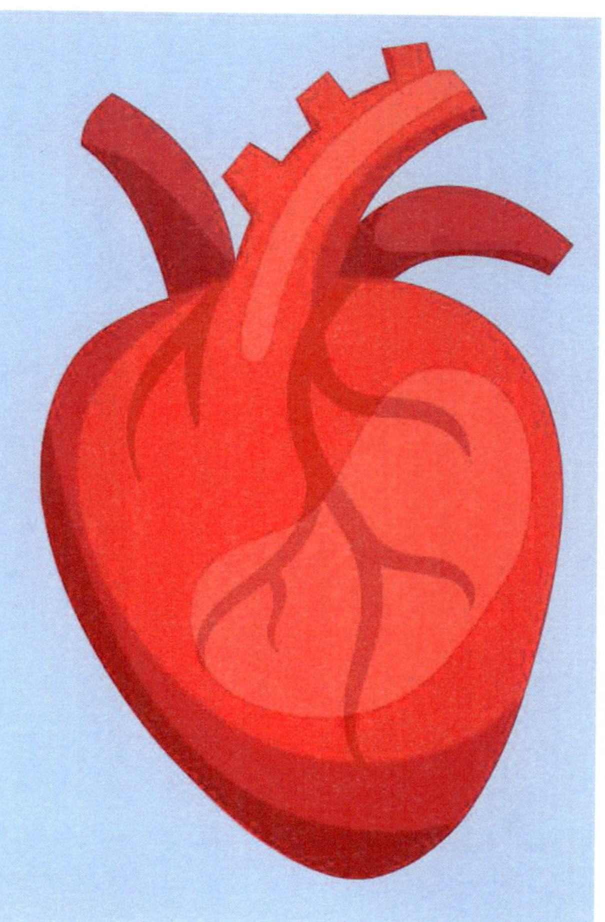

Having Congestive heart failure has made me pay close attention to what I put into my body that can ultimately affect my heart. Well, the same goes for the things that you allow to be stored up in your heart. What a man thinks in his heart flows out of his mouth. Let's take a moment and take inventory of your heart.

What source of nutrients are you using to feed to your heart.

What bad things are you allowing to settle in your heart?

Are you willing to allow God to soften your heart?

The type of soil you have will determine if the seeds we allow to be planted in us grow and become fruitful. These things can range from environments we place ourselves in, emotions that have lingered around too long and states of minds we have allowed ourselves to settle into. A state of mind can become permanent.

While a large crowd was gathering and people were coming to Jesus from town after town, he told this parable: "A farmer went out to sow his seed. As he was scattering the seed, some fell along the path; it was trampled on, and the birds ate it up. Some fell on rocky ground, and when it came up, the plants withered because they had no moisture. Other seed fell among thorns, which grew up with it and choked the plants. Still other seed fell on good soil. It came up and yielded a crop, a hundred times more than was sown."

– Luke 8:58

After doing some research one day on soil types I came upon 4 types of soils listed below. What blew my mind was how each soil lined up with this parable in the bible. Here's my breakdown of it.

The Four Types of Soil

<u>Silty Soil</u> -is slippery when wet, not grainy or rocky. **Silt** is created when rock is eroded, or worn away, by water and ice. To me this was like the first set of soil that the seeds got trampled on. This type of soil can represent the word solid. There was no place for the seed to plant itself, so it was trampled, then eaten up by birds. For example, some of you will read this book and you will hear the message and within moments something will come and distract you and steal these seeds away from you. This can be drama, social media, and etc., Be aware of the things that are here to come steal good things away from you. FRUITLESS!

<u>Clay Soil</u>-is a heavy soil type that benefits from high **nutrients**. Clay soils remain **wet** and cold in winter and dry out in summer. This soil is the rocky ground. This type of soil represents the word vulnerable. This soil was good enough to plant the seed and it grew, but what happens is because it gets no moisture it withers. Some of you will read this book and receive this message well, but as soon as opposition strikes, this message and this book will make its way to the back of the line…you know where you put all the things that could have meant something but the effort was too much of a sacrifice. It's like the moment you have to be vulnerable everything that you have worked hard for goes out the window. FRUITLESS!

Vulnerable- susceptible to physical or emotional attack or harm.

Sandy Soil - is light, warm, dry and tend to be acidic and low in nutrients. These **soils** have quick water drainage and are easy to work with. This is the soil that produces thorns. This represents the word congested. The soil was good enough to plant the seed and it grew. The best soil to produce thorn bushes is sandy soil, and what happens when thorns grow, is they can hinder other plants from growing. Some of you will read this book and receive the message well, but because there are so many things going on in your life you become consumed by the worries of the world. What I mean by that is, some of us are just too busy with things that nothing good can fit in. Some of us start to think that the more money we make, the less problems we will have or the busier we are, the less lonely we may feel. All of that is a worry that popular culture created for you. That turns into a desire in our hearts that was not placed there with good purpose and God's promise for you. You know what we end up doing with that cash? Spending it on something that will last for a moment, and we don't make any money off of it. What do we do when we've hung out with anyone and everyone that we can, only to distance ourselves because we think everyone is the problem? or, at least, get a good fulfilling memory off of it. That illustrates that when the plant gets choked out by the thorns, no fruit can be produced. And let's not forget that thorns hurt. FRUITLESS!

Loamy Soil-This soil is made with a balance of the three main types of **soil**: sand, silt, and clay **soil**. As a general rule, **loam soil** should consist of equal parts of all three **soil** types. This combination of **soil** types creates the perfect **soil** texture for plant growth.

For some, you will identify with one of the soils quickly and for most, it will be something that will take a little longer to recognize because you have been so focused on others' soil and not your own. Some of you are wondering why the person next to you has been more fruitful than you. It's because you both are functioning with different types of soil. I prefer the Loamy soil because I need to be able to grow, produce and multiply my fruit.

Once you have identified what type of soil you have, you can start to identify how your soil got like that to begin with.

What Type of Things Contribute to Feeding Your Soil?

I would describe it as anything we allow to deposit and/or reside into our hearts?

· Tv shows
· Quotes
· Memes
· Lack of discipline
· Perception
· Lack of understanding

· Environmental residue
· Lingering energy
· Spirits (of all kinds)
· Social media
· Books
· Radio
· Podcast
· Religion
· Influencers
· Old plants / leaves (your Past)
· And so on….

Lack of Knowledge About Our Soil

Being unaware of knowledge that you lack about your soil is a starter. This summer, I got a chance to learn a lot about plants because I fell in love with the "IDEA" of ways they could calm me and how they could add healthy benefits to my home. Let me add that these were the only things I looked up about the plants. The only things that were important to me were clean air and the Zen that was coming my way. I'm not quite sure why I limited myself about something that I was investing my time and money in, but I did.

Here are a few reasons why we block incoming knowledge from being received or sought out:

- Clinging to one's comfort zone.
- Fear of Failure.
- Arrogance
- Defensiveness.
- Impatience.
- Rigid mindset.
- Lack of perspective

Impatience and arrogance triggered me because I thought who ever couldn't take care of plants is an idiot and that all you have to do is water them, right? WRONG!

Lack of understanding

At this point, my house looked like little shop of horrors, but in a good way. My plan was to water the plants every day so that I would reap all the benefits (Yes, the only two I looked up). One plant started to die quickly while another plant flourished. They alternated in this pattern all over the house. I was aware that the plants were all different, but my lack of understanding prohibited me from creating separate plans for my plants. We typically lack understanding in things because we don't ask enough clarifying questions and/or we don't read the entire manual to begin with. I am guilty of both.

Lack of wisdom

Lack of wisdom comes from not having understanding or knowledge. Wisdom can't exist if you lack understanding of the information. Simple understanding doesn't come from compiling information in your head. It derives from identifying what words really mean and not the perceived definitions your brain has created. I can honestly admit to you, with a transparent heart, that I had acquired absolutely no wisdom about my plants prior to their downfall. What I can say is that my ego encouraged me to pretend like I had wisdom. It was really just to soothe an emotional need I was experiencing at the time and it was a costly one too. In the end, I wasted my money and my time because I chose arrogance and impatience over acquiring the wisdom. I chose opting into ego and opting out of humility. Please, **take the proper steps to gain wisdom. Lack of wisdom will always cost you!**

Lack of boundaries (excessive human demand of ourselves)

Buying 20+ plants was already excessive, but my capacity to care for the plants was limited. Not to be funny, but managing a hubby, two hormonal daughters, two dogs, and two baby companies, my capacity is full. If we offer ourselves up to people, events, activities, situations and so on with no limitation or boundaries for what we give out, we are setting ourselves up to damage our soil. For example, over watering or just putting a lot of unnecessary trinkets in your soil just to make it look busy.

I once heard a quote from Iyanla Vanzant that said, *"What is in your cup is for you. What comes out of your cup is for others."* Your cup cannot <u>runneth</u> over if you are allowing people to drink from inside the cup as well. If your cup isn't filling back up at the rate people are drinking from it, you are giving from an empty cup. You are essentially being disconnected from your gardener!

Bad Soil Can Reject a Good Seed!

At this moment in time we might be sitting here looking like, *"Well I'll be damned! When did this happen and how did we get here?"*

Our soil doesn't just become affected overnight. Soil can easily become damaged or toxic because it's not being carefully managed. If we understand our soil and manage it properly, we will avoid destroying one of the essential building blocks God has designed for ourselves and what feeds our spirits.

If you ignore the faulty state that your soil is currently in, your soil will eventually come destroy your tree.

"The ax is already at the root of the trees, and every tree that does not produce good fruit will be cut down and thrown into the fire."

-Matthew 3:10

Key Tips in Managing Your Soil

· **<u>Become aware of your soil</u>**- This is going to take some self-revelation, sometimes the ENEMY (Inner Me) is you!

· **<u>Take accountability for your faulty soil</u>** – Your soil is being managed by you and only you This can be no one else's fault but your own. Only you can change you! (+ GOD)

·**<u>Transplant yourself to some better soil</u>**- Sometimes it requires you to relocate, not necessarily physically, but spiritually. Your heart might need to be moved to a healthier pot of soil.

· **<u>Add some organic Compost</u>** – Or·gan·ic relating to or derived from living matter. This, for me, is the word of God, the manual for my life. For you, it might be something different, but you will need something organic to add nutrients back into your soil.

Here are a few keys things to know about the functionality and benefits of soil.

· Most plants get their nutrients from soil.
· It is the main source of survival.
· Most living things depend on soil for their existence.
· Soil Helps Anchor your roots.

"This is the meaning of the parable: The seed is the word of God. Those along the path are the ones who hear, and then the devil comes and takes away the word from their hearts, so that they may not believe and be saved. Those on the rocky ground are the ones who receive the word with joy when they hear it, but they have no root. They believe for a while, but in the time of testing they fall away. The seed that fell among thorns stands for those who hear, but as they go on their way they are choked by life's worries, riches and pleasures, and they do not mature. But the seed on good soil stands for those with a noble and good heart, who hear the word, retain it, and by persevering produce a crop."

-Luke 8:11-15

If you self-reflect regularly, you will have no problem acknowledging the things you mess up on because you're human. There is always room for error. You can immediately tell yourself that the mistakes made can be corrected. If you still allow yourself to settle for the excuses from your failures, your problems will continue to arise and become constant and consistent.

You can do a few things to prepare yourself to acquire the tools that I will give to you in each chapter of this book.

- ***Define your Core Values***

Core values are essential for personal development because they help you make wise decisions that will work in your favor to play on your strengths, wants, and needs. You must keep your core values in mind to help you achieve your goals when looking at your development path. Without reflecting upon your values, you will react to circumstances by making careless decisions that will hold you back in the long run.

- o *What are your core values?*
- o *Where did these core values come from? (Did they come preloaded or programmed, or did you create them to customize your lifestyle?)*
- o *What are things that you truly value in life? Write them down and reflect on them.*

Core Values Word List

Determine your core values. From the list below, choose and write down every core value that resonates with you. Do not overthink your selections. As you read through the list, write down the words that feel like a core value to you personally. If you think of a value you possess that is not on the list, be sure to write it down as well.

Abundance	Daring	Intuition	Preparedness
Acceptance	Decisiveness	Joy	Punctuality
Accountability	Dedication	Kindness	Relationships
Achievement	Dependability	Knowledge	Reliability
Advancement	Diversity	Leadership	Resilience
Adventure	Empathy	Learning	Resourcefulness
Advocacy	Encouragement	Love	Responsibility
Ambition	Enthusiasm	Loyalty	Responsiveness
Appreciation	Ethics	Making a Difference	Security
Attractiveness	Excellence	Mindfulness	Self-Control
Autonomy	Expressiveness	Motivation	Selflessness
Balance	Fairness	Optimism	Simplicity
Being the Best	Family	Open-Mindedness	Stability
Benevolence	Friendships	Originality	Success
Boldness	Flexibility	Passion	Teamwork
Brilliance	Freedom	Performance	Thankfulness
Calmness	Fun	Personal Development	Thoughtfulness
Caring	Generosity	Proactive	Traditionalism
Challenge	Grace	Professionalism	Trustworthiness
Charity	Growth	Quality	Understanding
Cheerfulness	Flexibility	Recognition	Uniqueness
Cleverness	Happiness	Risk Taking	Usefulness
Community	Health	Safety	Versatility
Commitment	Honesty	Security	Vision
Compassion	Humility	Service	Warmth
Cooperation	Humor	Spirituality	Wealth
Collaboration	Inclusiveness	Stability	Well-Being
Consistency	Independence	Peace	Wisdom
Contribution	Individuality	Perfection	Zeal
Creativity	Innovation	Playfulness	
Credibility	Inspiration	Popularity	
Curiosity	Intelligence	Power	

Gather Your Values

Group all similar values together from the list of values you just created. Group them in a way that makes sense to you, personally. Create a maximum of four groupings. If you have more than four groupings, drop those least important.
See the example below

Acceptance Compassion Inclusiveness Intuition Kindness Love Making a Difference Open-Mindedness Trustworthiness Relationships	Appreciation Encouragement Thankfulness Thoughtfulness Mindfulness Balance Health Personal Development Spirituality Well-being	Abundance Growth Wealth Security Freedom Independence Flexibility Peace	Cheerfulness Fun Happiness Humor Inspiration Joy Optimism Playfulness

Your Turn

Choose one word within each grouping that best represents the label for the entire group. Again, do not overthink your labels. There are no right or wrong answers. You are defining the answer that is right for you.

- **Get to know and understand your personality and who you are!**
  - *Either dispose of how you have been acting or EMBRACE who you are and run with that shit!*
  - *What are five traits that define you?*
  - *What are five words that describe you?*
  - *What role do you play in your tribe? (your group of friends)*
  - *If you were to meet someone, what would they have to say about you based on their first impression of you? * This doesn't mean the fake you. I mean the real you.*
  - *Do you speak when you see people you don't know? Are your kind to strangers?*
  - *What is your disposition when no one is watching?*

Character Traits List

Determine your character traits. From the list below, choose and write down every character trait that resonates with you. Do not overthink your selections. As you read through the list, simply write down the words that feel like character traits to you personally. If you think of a trait you possess that is not on the list, be sure to write it down as well.

Demanding
Thoughtful
Keen
Happy
Disagreeable
Simple
Fancy
Plain
Excited
Studious
Inventive
Creative
Thrilling
Intelligent
Proud
Fun-loving
Daring
Bright
Serious
Funny
Humorous
Sad
Lazy
Dreamer
Helpful
Simple-minded
Friendly
Adventurous
Timid
Shy
Pitiful
Cooperative

Lovable
Ambitious
Quiet
Curious
Reserved
Pleasing
Bossy
Witty
Energetic
Cheerful
Smart
Impulsive
Humorous
Sad
Lazy
Dreamer
Helpful

What are five traits that define you ?

GOD'S PROMISE

Direction
Trust in the Lord with all your heart
and lean not on your own understanding;
in all your ways submit to him,
and he will make your paths straight

Proverbs 3:5-6

THE TIFFANATOR

Talk to God

This is one of the easiest things to do because it's just like journaling but with a purpose and person in mind.

Chapter 3

Metal Detector - Being Intentional

You might be wondering what we need this for. Well, keep reading? Before entering this chapter, the backpack is required and necessary to carry all the tools we are going to use during this discovery. Every chapter, I will gift you a tool to help you out. You're welcome.

A metal detector is an electronic instrument that detects the presence of metal nearby. Metal detectors are useful for finding metal inclusions hidden within objects or metal objects buried underground. They often consist of a handheld unit with a sensor probe swept over the ground or other objects.

Toxins are easily detected when using something that is created to spot them out for you. We will call this the Toxin Detector. This tool will help us locate areas in our lives that we need to uncover and re-examine. The metal detector will allow us to find stuff that is buried deep beyond the surface. It can pick up toxins that have attached themselves to everyday things that we have purposely overlooked or unintentionally ignored. So, gear up. Let us detect some stuff!

Please make sure that you charge this up before each discovery. Let me explain what being charged up look likes.

1. Rest- You will need adequate rest for this journey, so please don't skip your sleep.
2. Nutrients- You will need to make sure you're taking your vitamins – or stop by your nearest juice shop (Intentions Juice Bar in Tacoma, Washington, is my fave!)
3. Outlet- Buy a journal and prep your nearest best friend. Your best friend may change throughout this process and what I mean by that is, you might have to become God's bestie first.

"Intentional living is the art of making our own choices before other choices make us."

To be intentional means to be done on purpose, to be deliberate.

You might ask the question, *"What if I don't know what my intent is because I have no idea what my purpose is?"*

Finding your purpose can be a challenging task if you're already off course. I believe that when you intentionally begin to live God's way, you will find it. To live God's way, you must ask Him to be your boo thang (check yes or yes). He checked yes for you, eons ago.

Secure but Insecure

I remember feeling so secure in myself but insecure in my identity. Could it be possible for both security and insecurity to coexist within you? I say absolutely! I was confident in how I looked, secure with my abilities, and content with my performance as a mother and a wife. I wasn't secure in my identity, though. Like really, who was Tiffynee? I had survived many near-death experiences, yet the revelation was still distant. After sitting back and looking over the events and activities that I had participated in throughout my life, I had to have a challenging moment of realization. I had wasted a lot of my time and efforts fulfilling unreasonable expectations I allowed others to place on me, not excluding myself. The things I sought out to accomplish had more to do with pleasing people and less to do with God's purpose for my life. Wait, are you saying I was walking around here living with no purpose? YES! SIS, IT WAS ME! It's crazy to think that 34 years had sailed by, and I was running on empty. When your spirit lacks the right food to fuel you, you're as good as a person who says things like this, *"I'll take $2.00 on Pump # 2"*, with gas at $2.89. Sis, you pull out of the gas station, and the gaslight has come right back on. Yes, that was me at one point!

3 STEPS

To figure out my purpose, I had to make a few decisions immediately.

01

Decide where you want to receive your information .

02

Decide if you are going to be intentional with seeking God's purpose for your life.

03

Decide when and how to start.

To figure out my purpose, I had to make a few immediate decisions.

1. Decide where I wanted to receive my information.

"Before I formed you in the womb I knew you, and before you were born I consecrated you; I appointed you a prophet to the nations." -Jeremiah 1:5

Think about it. If you're a believer, you know that God created you and then gifted you to your mother to birth you (for all you technical readers). We often expect that our parents know all the answers, especially about us, because we came from their DNA. T-Mobile sells iPhones, but when they malfunction, we contact Apple Care. It's the manufacturer you call to help you troubleshoot it. The best person to explain to you what your purpose is the Manufacturer (GOD!), not me and not anyone else!

2. Decide if I was going to be intentional with seeking God's purpose for my life.

Once you find out what the answer is, it is up to you to decide if you will apply it to your life or ignore it and carry on with your old habits. Well, I was undoubtedly over being insecure in my identity, so it was GAME TIME!

3. Decide when to start and how to start.

Starting something new is hard to do. I had to map out a plan. So, let me tell you what the Big Homie GOD did for me. One day, I was meditating, and I heard a "thirty-day fast."

Yes, that's all I heard. I'm looking around like, *"You can't be talking to me, SIR!"* Indeed, God had spoken and requested me to mute all my distractions for 30 days. Without hesitation, my intentionality popped in. I shut down my social media three days later. When God speaks to me, it is at a low vibration. Fasting is different for everyone. Some choose to fast from food, and some decide to fast from other things that serve as a sacrifice. For me, my sacrifice and distraction were social media. I felt that because He knows me well enough I'd quickly get distracted from what He is trying to show me. I had heard about the act of fasting for years and never really understood what it was and how it worked. To be honest, I thought people who fasted from food were silly until I saw, with my own eyes, its effect on someone else's life. That same year, a good friend of mine joined Lent for the first time. They struggled with weight loss and several health concerns throughout their entire lives. When they came to me and told me this was their plan, my initial thought was, this is so silly. Why would you starve yourself just for…? I couldn't understand, and their best way to describe what they were doing was that they needed to remove food from them because it distracted them from seeing what God had planned for them. It was a comfort for them. During those 40 days of lent, they went 100% at this and had terrific results afterwards: physically, mentally, and spiritually. So, when the Big Homie gave me similar directions, I didn't hesitate to oblige. His words were short and precise. I will say Social media was comforting to me, in addition to my friends. During the fast, everything that was comfortable to me was snatched from me, and God replaced it with Himself.

I needed to be intentional with seeking God and His purpose for my life no matter what and asking for clarification or making certain amendments to His request was out of the question. I tried once, and He demolished it, lol. I decided to remove myself from social media but still be a part of one thing that I had pre-committed to. I didn't want to disappoint anyone by removing myself for an unplanned but planned fast. As you can see, that didn't work. They say that God laughs when He sees your plans compared to His. Well, He got a good ol' chuckle. In the midst of me trying to accommodate that commitment I made, I got abruptly removed from it and not by my own doing. I'll explain more in volume two, Sis. Is it you? Realizing the Toxic in You. During this fiasco, my fast was extended by 15 days. It was clear that I had to complete 30 days of no social media. I thoroughly enjoyed it after a while.

It was necessary!

SIX WAYS TO BECOME
INTENTIONAL

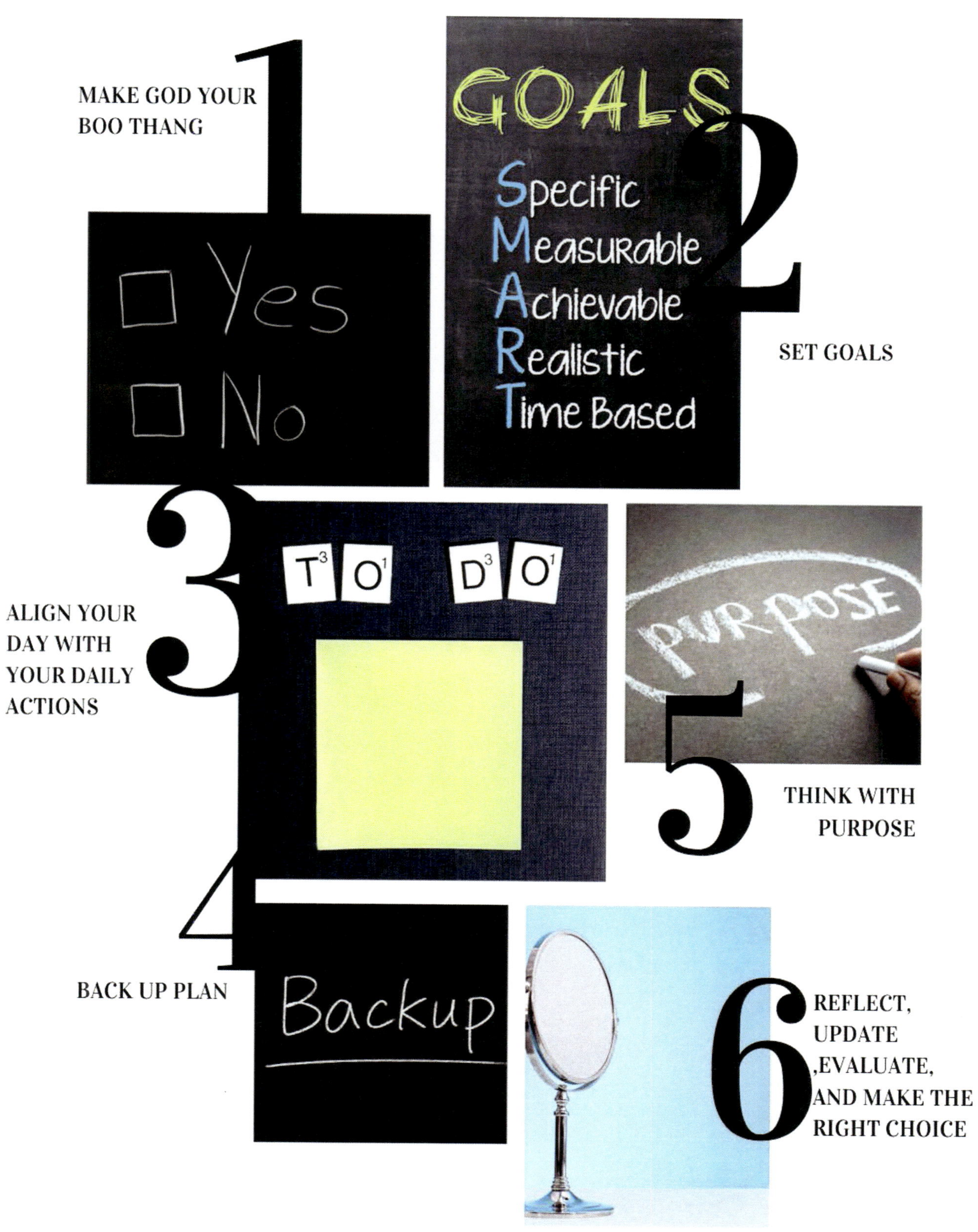

MAKE GOD YOUR BOO THANG
1
Yes
No
GOALS
Specific
Measurable
Achievable
Realistic
Time Based
2
SET GOALS
3
ALIGN YOUR DAY WITH YOUR DAILY ACTIONS
TO DO
PURPOSE
5
THINK WITH PURPOSE
4
BACK UP PLAN
Backup
6
REFLECT, UPDATE ,EVALUATE, AND MAKE THE RIGHT CHOICE

Step 1- Make God Your Boo Thang

The best way to get to know God is to discover His ways. Get to know His character, promises, and plans for you. It is just like forming a new relationship with anyone else. You have to talk to Him, aka investigate and interrogate, to find out all the tea. It's easy to judge somebody when you lack information about them and lack understanding of the information received. We are all guilty of this. Most of us were fed information from an unevolved religion or person. Just imagine getting to know him yourself. The more knowledge you receive about God, the more interested you will become about who He is, and the more you will desire to be His boo as well. A relationship with God is a unique but rewarding thing to have. I say this because, in this relationship, His only intent is for you to live a purposeful life. He only wants the best for you. His only requirement for you is to give your whole heart to Him, and He will take care of you. Aren't you tired of babysitting something that doesn't belong to you? Sis, give back your heart, please?

Naturally, a relationship like this takes time, patience, and willingness to change. I'm talking about the type of change where you have to re-position your heart where nothing flows from it but unconditional love. Having a relationship with God helps you grow as a person mentally, physically, and spiritually. Just imagine waking up every day, and your body is growing, but you still have the mindset of a child. Adulthood has nothing to do with the matriculation of your age or how your body looks. Meaning, just because you look the part doesn't mean you can play the role.

When I was a child, I talked like a child, I thought like a child, I reasoned like a child. When I became a man, I put the ways of childhood behind me.
1st Corinthians 13:11 NIV

Let's put the child's way of thinking behind us and adopt a new way of thinking. Think back to the ways God was introduced to you and calculate your level of understanding at that time compared to now. Give yourself credit for your growth thus far. A relationship with God can be comfortable if we focus more on what flows from the inside than outside. Many get caught up on if they can see God or not. That's the outside. God guides us through His Word. The gentle sound we hear are His instructions. He also gives signals through the Holy Spirit. That comes from the inside and then shows up on the outside, so if you're having trouble seeing Him, evaluate yourself.

Now, for all you Bible thumpers (Person/persons known to disqualify anything the bible says) that don't believe that the Word was written with good intent and have a problem with religion, causing a disconnect between God and you, I would ask for permission to show you something, but this is my book, so, I'll take you to some scripture.

"All scripture is God's breath and is useful for teaching, rebuking, correcting, and training and righteousness, so that the servant of God may be thoroughly equipped for every good work."
-2nd Timothy 3:16-17

To me, the Bible is a book of stories written from people's experiences with God. It's a book that tells us stories about how the Big Homie shows up and shows out, and history repeats itself. My suggestion to anyone reading this book is to dispose of those negative thoughts and connotations that religion has brought you. The Word of God gives those that can deliver it to wherever He intends it needs to be. Have you ever wondered why when you hear a sermon, and you say, *"OMG, why is this speaking to me right now?"* The message isn't new, but its purpose aligns divinely with where you are at any time in your life.

It's God's Word that is teaching us to do right. It's about having a spiritual connection with Him and giving Him full reign to use you according to His purpose. I pose this question: why are there so many books written about this one book? Whether it be to deny it or to agree with it, this book, "The Bible", is fruitful.

Do not be conformed to this world but be transformed by the renewing of your mind. By testing, you may discern what the will of God is, what is good and acceptable and perfect.
-Romans 12:2

Think about everything that's going on in the world today: the good, bad, and the ugly. We can all agree that the things we got to see, and experience were not all the ways of God. Now use the gift of discernment (we discussed this earlier) and listen to His specific instructions.

Now that we've gotten a little up close and personal with our Lord and Savior (Clap one time for your BOI), the following steps require more work. God being your boo was a given.
He has been dating you before you started dating Him!

Sort it Out!

Getting to know God's Promises.

So try to dispose of those negative thoughts or connotations that religion has brought you.

Romans 12:2 says, Do not be conformed to this world, but be transformed by the renewing of your mind. By testing, you may discern what is the will of God, what is good and acceptable and perfect.

Write a list of thoughts that you currently hold about the following topics. Place your thoughts in the appropiate can.

Step 2- Set Goals

*A goal is an idea of the future or desired result that a person or group of
people envision, plan, commit to achieving.*

To be intentional, you have to incorporate goal setting into your daily life. Setting goals gives you daily purpose and helps you guide your life and keep it on track. They show you where you want to go, but it's still on you to choose the path and stick to the way to get there.

I set a goal to get intentional with my Bible app, and the goal was to read my Bible app every day and absorb what I was reading, to meditate on it and understand it. This goal was not hard to set because the You Version Bible app has daily devotionals every day, and they added streaks. I just recently learned about streaks. My oldest kept bragging about her streaks she was having on snap chat, and I wasn't feeling the word, but I also recognize I'm not as hip to the new definitions of words, so I looked it up. A streak happens when you interact with the app within 24 hours for more than three consecutive days.
To gain a sense of accomplishment and to reward your brain, they created streaks. Every day you got a streak, and it would increase the more you remained faithful to it. For me, this became a little addicting, but in a good way. I wanted to challenge myself to get a good streak going.

You might be thinking, what does this have to do with discovering my self-revelations? You want to have an easier time self-evaluating, so you have to be deliberate in doing so as often as you can. If being your best self is what's most important to you, you're going to have to get uncomfortable with the old you and get in the habit of correcting yourself. That's your number one goal: CHANGE! God explains why it's so important to set goals. This parable from the handy dandy Bible will give you a playful look at how all God's creatures plan.

You lazy fool, look at an ant.
Watch it closely; let it teach you a thing or two.
Nobody has to tell it what to do.
All summer, it stores up food;
At harvest, it stockpiles provisions.
So how long are you going to laze around doing nothing?
How long before you get out of bed?
A nap here, a nap there, a day off here, a day off there,

Sit back, take it easy—do you know what comes next?
Just this: You can look forward to a dirt-poor life,
Poverty your permanent houseguest!

Proverbs 6:6-11 MSG

If ants can make it happen, why can't you?

Trying to measure your goals without structure can throw you off track, so I took something I learned in almost every college course I have taken. I also apply this with my clients. It's called SMART.

SMART is an acronym created to map out your goals and make them attainable. Your goals need to be **Specific, Measurable, Attainable, Relevant, And Time-Based.** I like to use smart goals when I keep saying I'm going to complete something, and I don't. It's the planning for me! I hate planning because it requires me to work harder than I originally intended to, but when I plan, I avoid unnecessary chaos. Many of you will look at this activity below with the same thought process I have had since I originally learned it. It's useless, and just another thing for me to do when I don't have time to do the stuff I already have to do. And if you're identical to me, you will have it anchored in your head that this is something you will skip. Sis, we all use this acronym without even knowing it and where we apply it directly. It works so well it has allowed us to succeed in a few things in life. We plan our time very effectively when it comes to just one simple thing, like waking up and going to bed.

 If you're like me, you don't like to be awakened before the planned time that you created in your head before you laid down. Very few of us wake up when we feel like it. It is something that we plan. Hello! What do you think alarms were created for? That's intentional planning. When I plan the time that I'm going to wake up, I use smart goals unconsciously. Look at the example I detailed out below.

DAILY SMART GOALS

Wake Up

S — Specific: To get Jai up for school on time.

M — Measurable: Setting the alarm 30-10-5 will help me cope with having to get up.

A — ACHIEVABLE: If I set the alarm, I will get up.

R — REALISTIC: Putting the phone near my ear and setting 3 alarms will ensure I get up.

T — TIME-BASED: I need to wake up by 7am.

Go to Bed

S — Specific: I need to go to bed by at least 1:30 so I can get 5 plus hours of sleep.

M — Measurable: Taking the sleep aid 1.5 hours prior to my cut off time will help me get to bed.

A — ACHIEVABLE: Turning off the Tv. .

R — REALISTIC: Turning off the Tv. .

T — TIME-BASED: I need to go to bed by 1:30am.

Purpose: Wake up and go to bed

Realistically, we all do this in is some kind of form, and by the end of this book you will be able to see clearer that the principles and promises you align with, were presented in an old way and I'm just here to represent things.

SMART GOALS

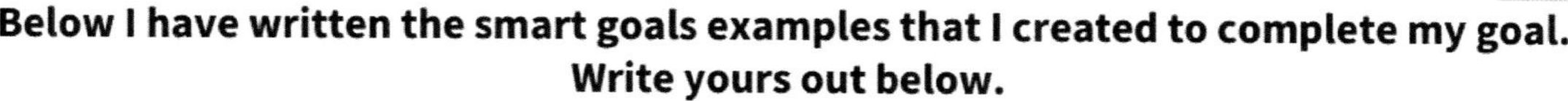

**Below I have written the smart goals examples that I created to complete my goal.
Write yours out below.**

Specific

Who, What, When, Where, and Why
Read my bible every day

Measurable

How will I know when it is accomplished?
Completing at least One Daily Devotional and consecutively participating in an active devotional plan.

Achievable

Is the goal within your reach?
There is 1440 min in a day. It only takes 5 - 7 minutes to complete the devotional. 2 devotionals = about 14 minutes.

Realistic

Are you willing to do the work?
I have more than 14 minutes of my time to spare and I'm not on social media right now.

Time-Based

Time frame?
July 6th - August 25th ,2020

Get A Vision

Most people will use vision boards to help them identify and visualize their goals. It is imperative that you see the things that you are striving for every day. In order to get a vision, you are going to need to map it out.

For self- Self is first because self is the being who is going to make all the rest of this happen. Don't confuse this with being selfish. You can't give from an empty cup.

For Family- These are the things you want to do that will ultimately contribute to your legacy. Your family is a part of that fruit God talks about when He says be fruitful and multiply. What things are in your vision and a part of your plans that will contribute to your legacy?

For Finances- Your finances are what help contribute to the type of life you want to live. Planning these things allow you to see how you will apply yourself and multiply your fruit. Yes, I said yourself. Whatever gift that God gave you, it was intended to be fruitful. Yes, that means make money…however that may look for you.

For Future- Your future is your legacy. What you see in the future is something great and in order to get there successfully, you must have a vision of what it looks like.

These Four categories are just examples of how to map out your vision. If you look below you can see my vision board.

My Vision

These Four categories are just examples of how to map out your vision. If you look below you can see my vision board.

For Self

- Focus
- Tools
- Evolve
- Awaken
- Detox
- Joy
- Discipline
- Toxic
- Self-Revelation
- Inspire
- Growth
- Embrace
- Change

For Family

- Organization
- Restructuring
- Therapy
- Vacation
- Growth
- Intimacy
- Disruption

For Finance

- Financial planning
- Income
- Increase
- Retreats
- Sis is it you
- Couples Boot camp

For Future

- Speaking Engagements
- Traveling the world
- Real Estate
- Expansion

VISION BOARD 2021
Discipline
JOY
FOCUS
Follow
ONE
Course
Until
Successful
EVOLVE
AWAKEN
LEARN
EVOLVE
TRANSFORM
BECOME
performance
results
SOLUTIONS
TEAMWORK
ORGANIZATION
services
career
sales
MANAGEMENT
STRATEGIES
MARKETING
support
leadership
DESTROY
WHAT
DESTROYS
YOU
Restructuring
DETOX
TOXIC
EMBRACE
CHANGE
inspire
be inspired
GROWTH
SELF
Revelation
seven golden stands
24
FINANCIAL PLAN
OVERCOMING
COMMUNICATION
CHALLENGES:
5 STEP GUIDE
Sis is it You
Tiffynee Terry Thomas
profit
HELLO
Bonjour
Ciao
Hola
HOUSTON
Galveston
DISCOVERING
SELF
REVELATION
Tiffynee
Terry-Thomas
FOR
SALE
RETREATS
COUPLES
&
INDIVIDUAL
BOOTCAMP
EXPANSION

The purpose of creating a vision board is not to be aesthetically pleasing or to match the décor in your room. If you're looking to place it in your nice decorated room and it doesn't quite go with the vibe, my suggestion would be to put it somewhere that you don't mind looking at it every day (closet, bathroom, etc.), as long as it's still somewhere in your line of sight. My most straightforward suggestion would be to make a digital one and put it as your screensaver. I would also suggest that you join or create an accountability group and create vision boards every six months—an excellent tool to use to help you stay on track.

The Vision

Most people will use vision boards to help them identify and visualize their goals. It might be a good idea for you to join a group and create vision boards every six months—an excellent tool to use to help you stay on track.
Write out your vision for the upcoming year.
Let's Manifest Good Things!

For Self	**For Family**
For Finance	**For Future**

God explains why it's so important to set goals.
You lazy fool, look at an ant.
Watch it closely; let it teach you a thing or two.
Nobody has to tell it what to do.
All summer, it stores up food;
At harvest, it stockpiles provisions.
So how long are you going to laze around doing nothing?
How long before you get out of bed?
A nap here, a nap there, a day off here, a day off there,
Sit back, take it easy—do you know what comes next?
Just this: You can look forward to a dirt-poor life,
Poverty your permanent houseguest!
Proverbs 6:6-11 MSG

Are you going to let the Ant out plan you ?

Setting and planning your goals will require you to break things down into micro-steps, so that you don't become overwhelmed by the outcomes and stay mindful throughout the process. You will have to ask yourself a few helpful questions to help you sort out your plans. One of my main goals was to get to know God more intimately. In order to do that, I needed to set a goal to have morning devotion every day for at least 30 days straight. Below are just a few examples of how you can seek to reach your goals. My grandfather always used to say, *"If you fail to plan, then you plan to fail."*

Every day make a to-do list to help you get things done to set intentionally. So, use what man gave us and jot it down because you cannot remember everything.

The Plan

Setting goals gives you daily purpose and helps you guide your life and keep it on track. They show you where you want to go, but it's still on you to stick to the path to get there.
To get to a destination, you must create a plan on how to get there.

Ask yourself these following questions:

Where are you going?

How will you get there?

What are you taking with you?

What are you willing to leave behind?

Once you get there, how will you contribute that to the world and make the most of it?

Step 3 -Align Your Day with Your Daily Actions

Make a "TO DO LIST!"

Most often, we fail to get to the intent of things because we fail to make a step-by-step plan for our goal. Map it out to visualize what it looks like and make sure that your day follows all the steps to achieve the goals you set. There are effective ways to create a do list, and you might be thinking about how hard it is to make a to-do list. It's not hard to create one, but the level of difficulty heightens when you compare that to completing everything on it or having any sense of accomplishment. Your list should encompass a few foundational qualities such as the following:

Being Effective

To be effective, you will need to make sure that you create a system that helps you maintain and manage this list. You can download apps to your phone or use paper and pen. The choice is yours to make. Whatever you choose, it needs to be with you during the duration of completing these daily goals. It needs to have mobility. I have used apps like Any Do, Tasks, Trello, and good old fashion paper and pen.

Being Efficient

To be efficient, you will need to assign due dates and limit the task you set yourself every day. It keeps you up to date with everything and gives you just enough to accomplish daily without feeling burnt out. Sometimes I find it harder to come up with a date of completion than the actual task itself. When I took the time to sit down and look at my schedule, I got a better look at what was going on in my life. I get anxious having to commit to anything, and not knowing if I'm going to feel up to something makes me nervous. Sis, I have commitment issues. Letting people down doesn't make me happy. So, once I commit to something, I know that I have to show up or else. That's why creating a list is hard for me. I understand that those are the things I have to do. Once it is on paper, I can no longer be blind to what needs to be done.

Be Fulfilling

To be fulfilled, you will need to make sure you keep your goals, objectives, and tasks separate. Keeping these separate helps you not become overwhelmed with significant results and keeps you focused on the process. As you complete the to-do list, you will feel an immediate sense of accomplishment and want to do it again the next day. Your objective is the end goal. My overall goal was to read my bible 14 minutes out of the day for a month straight. Me signing up for the devotionals was a task. The goal was to complete them. Separating them allowed me not to become overwhelmed by everything at once. The objective is the destination. The tasks are the vehicle and guidance to get there.

Being Beneficial

A good to-do list should serve as a benefit to you, not a burden. As you start to compile a list, keep in mind that you need to understand that prioritizing the list has to be your primary focus. Weeding out the non-important tasks and grouping things together will help you move items to the appropriate list. All objectives will differ, but it's essential to be able to notice the difference. Sometimes, I would catch myself doing to most unimportant stuff and allowing important things to pile up or vice versa. Sometimes nothing would get done. This happens more often than I would like to admit. I lacked the basic skills of prioritizing things. This is something that may come easy to some, but for others, it may be a difficult task because everything is important to them. Let me tell you, I believe that many devotional plans are essential to read, but I know I can't read them all. The word *all* is too heavy for one person to carry, so do yourself a favor and do some bit by bit and create a plan.

Types of list needed

You will need to make a few lists to fulfill all of the qualities above. LISSSTTTTTSSSS (Soulja Boy's Voice) You will not need to use each of these lists daily, but you need them to help you sort out and prioritize everything.

- Brain Dump List- Anything and everything goes on this list. This list is to empty your brain, so you can sort and prioritize your tasks.
- To-do list- This list will consist of things you can complete each day (limit to 2-5 tasks).
- Priority List- This list will consist of things that are a priority to get done. You can delegate these tasks throughout the week to yourself.

As you continue down this path, your reasoning becomes a comfortable weight to carry because there was never a plan from the beginning. You will consistently justify your excuses and will never create any positive results. When we have no plans to go anywhere, and we are given the opportunity to check something out last minute, and something interferes with us going, we usually don't care. If we plan something out…clothes, hair, makeup, nails, and so on, and plans get canceled, we are pissed. Want to know why? Because we put some thought into doing something. We spent time, energy, and money, and it didn't go as planned. Well, if you align yourself daily with the plans you made, you're going to take accountability for being intentional. If you adapt to this habit of planning, you will eventually become adamant about being successful every day. Being intentional about self-revelation is not an easy task when you lack planning skills. So, let's make a plan to be deliberate about this discovery we are about to go on.

Today's To Do List

Making a to-do list every day to help you get things done will help you set intentional goals daily. The human mind was not created to remember everything; So use what I'm giving you and jot it down!

Today's To Do List Breakdown

Now take what you just wrote down above and lets break it down and make it doable.

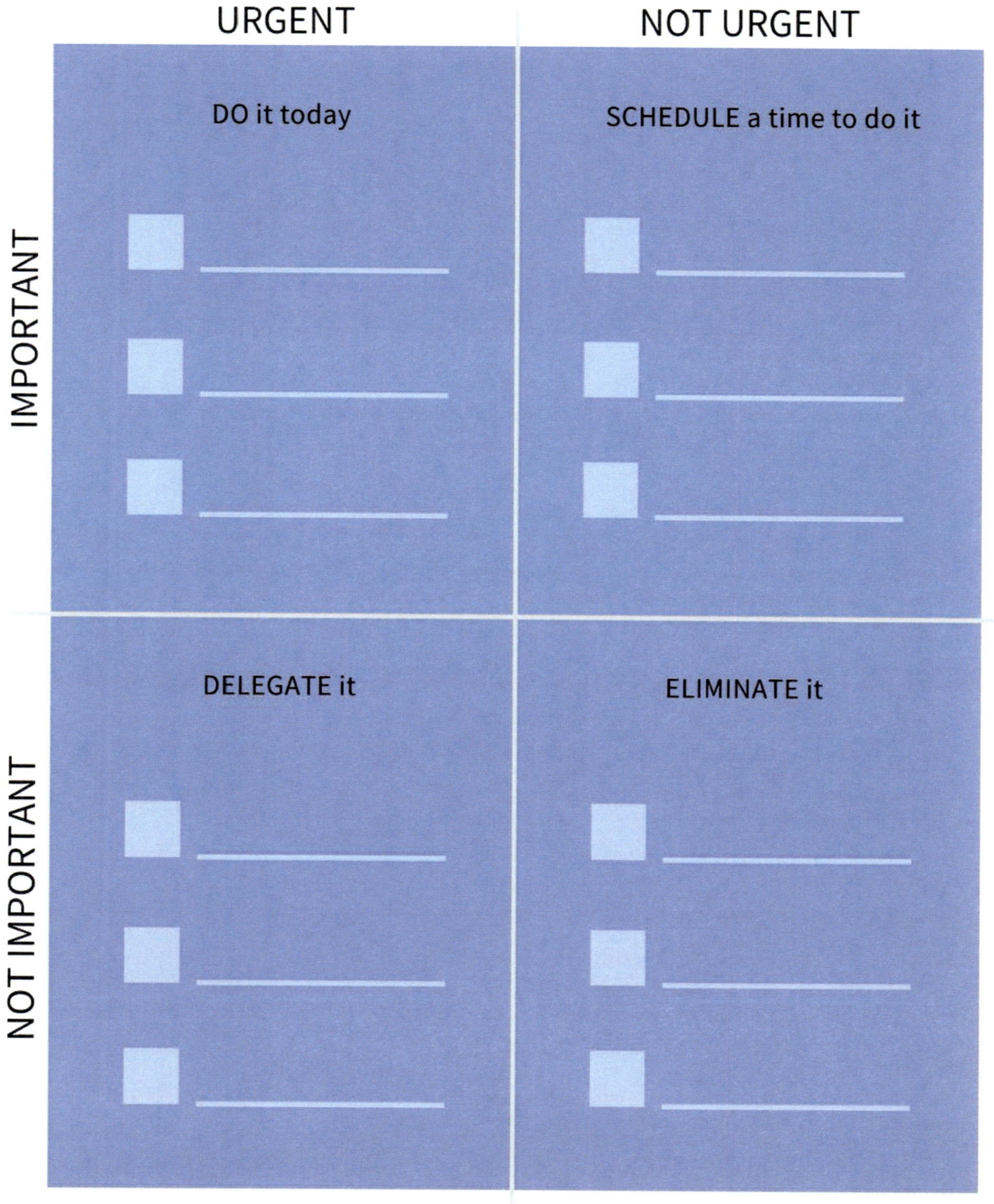

Step 4- The Back-Up Plan

I can guarantee that someday you will not want yourself to do something you're supposed to do. If you don't have a backup plan, you will be planning to fail.

Fight all of your Mind Monsters with every resource available to you.

Mind monsters are the negative thoughts we battle daily. These mind monsters can annihilate you with no remorse. I picture it like this: mind monsters are throwing a rave party in your head, and all of its guests are pessimistic thoughts. They creep into your head when you're not paying attention and have an "ALL ACCESS PASS" to your past mistakes.

Jesus told this simple story, but they had no idea what he was talking about. So he tried again. "I'll be explicit, then. I am the Gate for the sheep. All those others are up to no good—sheep rustlers, every one of them. But the sheep didn't listen to them. I am the Gate. Anyone who goes through me will be cared for—will freely go in and out and find pasture. A thief is only there to steal and kill and destroy. I came so they can have real and eternal life, more and better life than they ever dreamed of.

-John 10:10 MSG

Mind Monsters

If you have mind monsters walking freely in your mind, you cant think with purpose. It can lead you to a lot of places that you don't want to be. Mind Monsters can invade your mind and take you to places that you never wanted to go to.

List out all the mind monsters your dealing with.

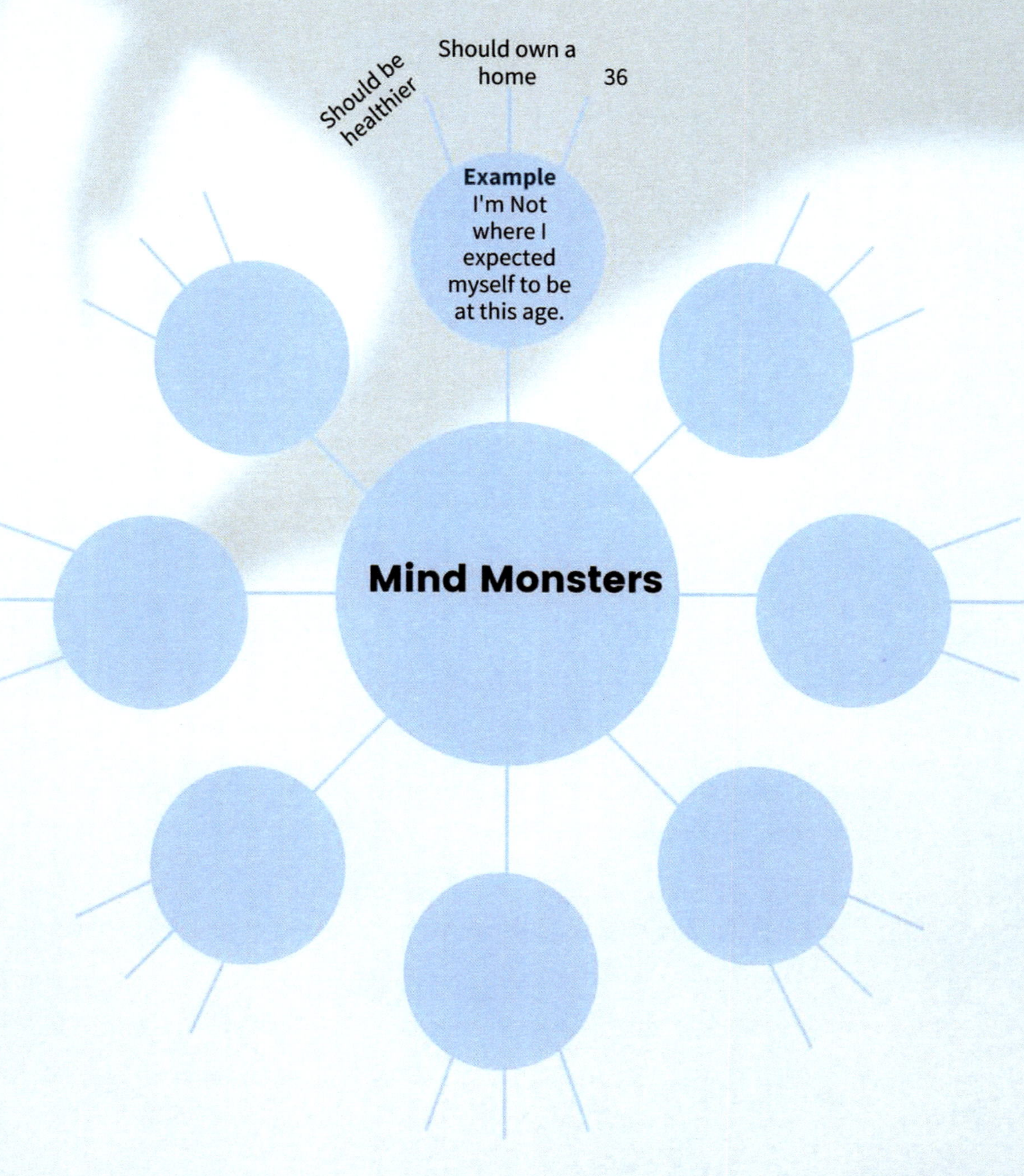

There are so many forces working hard to make sure that whatever God promised to you doesn't come to pass. While writing this book, I have had to push pause a few times because of Mind Monsters. Mine came in the form of anxiety. Do you know how hard it is to write and book and then have to go back and re-read it 50 million times? I sometimes would talk myself out of just going into my office to work on one chapter a day. I would find any excuse to help me avoid finishing this book. My mind would create things that didn't even or exist, or it would allow me to forget things to hinder my moving forward.

Politely take your pass back!

Practicing mindfulness will be essential during this process of battling your Mind Monsters. When your mind is full of junk, it's hard to stay positive with yesterday's garbage stinking up your space. Staying mindful keeps you in the present moment and acknowledges the here and now. I do not recommend battling these by yourself. Never isolate yourself when these thoughts become too overwhelming. Mental illness is real and it affects us all. If you struggle with these thoughts and they seem to overload your brain, please seek a professional to help with tips and techniques to improve your thoughts. Here are a few suggestions:

· Coaching

· Counseling

· Sermons (YouTube: P. Moody P. Todd, P. Keion, P.Furtick, TD Jakes, Sarah Jakes, Priscilla Shirer, and many more.)

· Meditation

Commitment is promising yourself that you will do it no matter what. It is more than merely telling yourself that you will do something.

Trust me, it is easy to get discouraged, and the temptation of giving up will cross your mind when you're having a bad day. Creating a backup for moments like these would be beneficial to your success of being intentional. This plan should incorporate the promise of making the day somewhat productive. Reaching out to one of your strong community members (mentioned in Chapter 6) to help you stay accountable will help you manage yourself as well. Changing your mindset from being completely lazy and wasting the day away to making sure that you at least accomplish one thing today will be your main objective. You are showing up despite how you feel because you're intentional about this discovery. A simple headache can take me off the course of my path, and I immediately become incapable of completing anything because the pain in my head binds me to my bed.

My mother called me one day, and I told her that I had recently been experiencing these terrible headaches for the past few days, but I failed to mention that I had forgotten to take my blood pressure medicine for more than a couple of days. My mother said to me, *"You need to set the alarm to remind you to take your meds."*

She reminded me that to be intentional also means to be preventative of things. Yes, I'm aware that not taking my meds can lead to headaches and other life-threatening things. It's laziness. Lawd, help me. I need to be intentional in setting up reminders to take my medicine because I'm not going to remember.

Few Things to Remember

· Put it on the calendar.

· Set an alarm

· Write a sticky note to yourself.

My backup plan had a few layers to it. It took one more person from my strong community to say something to me before putting this plan into full action. While trying to hold my daughter accountable for something, I was on the phone with my best friend. I repeated to her what I had just said to my daughter, "and then I proceeded to say, *"I'm mean, why can she be consistent? I am consistent, right?"*

My best friend replied, *"Be more specific? There are things that you're not consistent in, like taking your medicine every day."*

Sis, she was absolutely right about that. For me, when someone calls me out, I don't like it. I don't like it so much that I immediately start trying to fix myself. I ordered a 30-day planner for my meds. I knew that when I had to go into each individual pill container every time for about 4-7 different meds, I was more likely not going to take it. If it were in one spot and all together, it would be easier for me to manage. Filling it up once a month also helped me not to forget and fall back into that habit.

THE BACK-UP PLAN

Step 5- Think with Purpose

Now, I want you to think with purpose. Did you know that to perform your best takes intentionality and deliberate effort? You can have all the tools and skills necessary. If you struggle with mastering your mind, that causes the disconnect in the process. When you don't think with purpose, you become reactive, which puts you at the mercy of your potential environments and circumstances. Before my self-discovery phase, this was a massive problem for me. I was insecure in my identity I lacked purpose. So, when it came to finishing this book, it was pertinent to become intentional with my thinking to kick this bad habit I had acquired along the way. When you can think with purpose, it increases your life in three distinct ways.

Confidence

Intentional thinking breeds confidence. It allows you to coach yourself to higher performance. Feeling like you're not good enough and then reacting by saying that you're unworthy will only reinforce those thoughts. When you intentionally think with purpose, you reverse those thoughts and replace them with God's promises.

"For we are God's handiwork, created in Christ Jesus to do good works,
which God prepared in advance for us to do."

-Ephesians 2:10

I noticed that every time I mentioned to someone that I wrote a book, they would inquire what the book was about. Once I got finished explaining the concept, I felt on fire all over again. It helped build my confidence when others would congratulate the idea and then say, *"I think I imma have to purchase that."* I could no longer shy away from what I was doing.

Consistency

Intentional thinking promotes consistency. You know what to expect from yourself. There are no surprises. Ensuring that you get the same effort, attitude, and performance consistently. Having the ability to think with purpose on purpose gives you predictable outcomes.

"And let us not grow weary of doing good, for in due season we will
reap, if we do not give up."

-Galatians 6:9

The more I tried to hide it, the more I pushed it to the side. The more I talked about it, the more I became more motivated to complete it. So, I became consistent with what pushed me to complete it. When people would ask me how I was doing during the day I would tell them how I was struggling trying to finish. They would, of course, say something uplifting such as *"Girl, I was just bragging about you. I can't wait till you finish, imma get my copy. "* People have no idea what type of encouragement they offer in moments of despair or just plain ol' burnout. I'm grateful for friends like this.

Control

Intentional thinking steers control. Being in the driver's seat allows you to guide yourself on the map God has set out for your life. Taking charge of your thoughts helps you manage your performance. It doesn't allow your circumstances to dictate your behavior or your temporary emotions.

> *"For God gave us a spirit, not of fear but power and love and self-control."*
>
> *-2 Timothy 1:7*

I think that it's easy to become addicted to control and power in the wrong way, but I also believe that having control over your thoughts doesn't mean that you never lose control. It can just mean that you are quick to recognize when you are starting to swerve on the road, and you need to gain control of the car. For me, this requires the person inside of me to have a strong voice and hand. If not, Sis, it's the loss of control for me. Controlling my thoughts during this book writing process hasn't been an easy task, but I have learned that it takes all the above to maintain this. I reminded myself that I was confident, that I was going to remain consistent, and that allowed me to remain in control. Boop!

THE POWER OF
YOUR THOUGHTS

Watch your thoughts.

Everybody says that your thoughts are powerful, but how powerful can they be? Well, from my experience, they can create the life you are currently living. The way we think dramatically influences the way we feel. If you have mind monsters walking freely in your mind, you can't think with purpose. It can lead you to a lot of places that you don't want to be.

Hype WO(man)

We have established that some people don't think with purpose because they are not sure of their purpose. As we go on this journey, we will learn ways to achieve that goal. To believe on purpose, you can use purposeful thoughts and affirmations to align yourself with your purpose. For me, I had to take a step back and evaluate my current thought pattern, which would enable me to see where I was, and from there, I could align where I needed to go. Your actions are ultimately controlled by how you think. I needed to hire a hype WO(man) and not externally, but internally. This hype WO(man) needed to have the following qualifications to get the job.

<u>Hype WO(man) Requirements</u>
- She must remind me to focus on the right things.
- She must keep me in the present.
- She must calm or be able to de-escalate my emotions.
- She must use positive reinforcement to patrol my mind.
- She must help me maintain my confidence.
- She must help me be proactive and preventative.
- She must be my extra set of eyes.

I had to promote the self-talker in me. She needed some guidance and some structure on what I needed to be successful. You have to acquire new skills and open to learning opened my ability to think with purpose. Reminding ourselves to continue to focus on the right things and being present in the moment will keep us on the right path. It is easy to become distracted and fall off the course designed to direct us to our destination. Calming and de-escalating your emotions will enable you to ease up on the heaviness of your thoughts. I found myself having to pick myself up off the ground sometimes because I would allow my emotions to run frivolously throughout my mind. Using positive reinforcement to patrol the streets of your mind keeps you in a proactive and preventative state of mind. The Hype WO(man) had to tell me frequently, *" We don't care about that."* She had mantras she would sing in my head. They became instrumental and powerful. Maintaining your confidence through all of this will allow you to stay strong even in brief moments of weakness. The Hype WO(man) helps my confidence become a force to be reckoned with.

*"As a **man** "**thinketh** in his heart, **so is he**."*

-Proverbs 23:7

MY DAY

GOALS

DATE:

TO DO

5AM

6

7

8

9

10

11

12PM

1

2

3

4

5

6

7

8

9

10

11

12AM

Step 6-Reflect, Update, Evaluate, and Make the Right Choice.

Reflect

After going through the first five steps to ensure that you will use these steps, take a moment to reflect. Self-reflection is a must, and it needs to be taken seriously and managed well. You must come to a point in your life where emotional intelligence and being proactively self-aware are always a top priority in your life. Stay hungry for God's word, and you're well on your way. Be intentional! As I got to this point in my life, it was time to be honest about the things I wasn't intentional about. To correct something, you must identify with the problem completely. Don't continue to say, *"Well, sometimes I'm intentional,"* and think that it's ok. It's NOT!

Just as water mirrors your face, so your face mirrors your heart.

-Proverbs 27:19

When I took a step back and evaluated my progress, I saw inconsistency through my progress. I noticed that there were long gaps between things, and there were many things that had gotten started, but from what I saw, very few things got completed. Was this what God intended for my life? To have a bunch of great ideas that He gave me and to not have any of them completed. I'm going to say that was a hard no! What had I accomplished?

Accomplish-to achieve or complete successfully.

When I took a good look at what I had accomplished, the list was short. There were very many tasks that I had achieved, but as far as finishing them all successfully, that once again was a hard no! That's when I had to be honest with myself. The most challenging question I had to ask myself was some of the critical learning moments I had that year. They all fell under a lack of planning and consistency. I experienced it even while writing this book. There were many times that I was required to take a step back and reflect on what I was doing. The last chapter in this book is called the table – reflections. When you put everything on the table, you can see what has and has not been done. You can reflect!

Update

Update yourself regularly. You must just upgrade yourself to a newer and better version of yourself after getting to know yourself. This brief conversation I had with a client was to illustrate how we avoid updating ourselves.

Me: *"How often do you power off your phone?"*

Client: *"Never I'm always on it."*

Me: *"When was the last time you had to update your phone?"*

Client: *"A few weeks ago."*

Me: *"What did that process look like, and can you explain it to me in detail?"*

Client: *"You have to go to the settings, scroll down to the general tab to see software updated, and press it. It takes a lot of power to update, so you will have to connect to a charger while updating it."*

Me: *"Can you use the phone while it's updating?"*

Client: *"No, NOT AT ALL!"*

Me: *"What do you use your phone for?"*

Client: *"To communicate with people, socialize, gather information, and kill time."*

Me: *"So, how long do your updates sit before you accept the update?"*

Client: *"For a while, it takes some time."*

Me: *"Does your phone ever act funny? (before the update)"*

Client: *"Yes."*

Me: *"What do you do when it does that?"*

Client: *"Reset it and power off and power on!"*

Client: *"Man, you're filthy with it."*

Me: *"Lol, what do you think I'm trying to say to you?"*

Client: *"That I need to update the way I operate and reset my thinking."*

You treat yourself like you treat your phone. Even though you are aware that updating means you need to allot time for recalibrating things and fixing any buggy issues your phone is experiencing, you chose to power it off. The convenience that we find in finding valuable and functional sources to nurse issues and problems temporarily consumes our valuable time. Yes, an update requires you to shut down for a short while, but you are now functioning as a better self when you power yourself back on.

During my 30 days fast, I was able to update myself. I would like to say by the looks of this book, I upgraded myself as well.

I must continually re-identify myself to myself, reactivate my own standards, my own convictions, about what I'm doing and why.
-Nina Simone

Evaluate

It's time to form an idea of where we go from here with our intentionality, and we must take all the information we acquired from this specific tool and apply it to our discovery. During the evaluation process, give yourself credit where it is due and allow conviction for change. Remember, your identity isn't based on what you do. It's based on your *who*. Your identity comes from God, and if you look with a concentrated eye and an open ear, He reveals His plan in His Word.

TIff Tip: If you're struggling with understanding God's word, reading the message version helps you better understand what He is trying to say to you!

MY WEEK

MON

TUE

WED

THU

FRI

SAT

SUN

DATE:

PRIORITIES

TO DO

TO DO

ACTION STEPS / PRIORITY TASKS

1.

2.

3.

REFLECTION

Self-reflection is a must, and it needs to be taken seriously while being managed well. You have to come to a point in your life where emotional intelligence and being proactively self-aware are always a top priority in your life. Be intentional. Stay hungry for God's word, and you're well on your way.

Write Down how you plan on applying intentionality to your life.

GOD'S PROMISE

Intentionality

Look carefully then how you walk, not as unwise but as wise, making the best use of the time, because the days are evil. Therefore, do not be foolish, but understand what the will of the Lord is. And do not get drunk with wine, for that is debauchery, but be filled with the Spirit, addressing one another in psalms and hymns and spiritual songs, singing and making melody to the Lord with your heart, giving thanks always and for everything to God the Father in the name of our Lord Jesus Christ, submitting to one another out of reverence for Christ.

Ephesians 5:15-21 ESV

w w w . s i s i s i t y o u . c o m

THE TIFFANATOR

Talk to God

This is one of the easiest things to do because it's just like journaling but with a purpose and person in mind.

CHAPTER 4

PIN POINTER - HAVE HUMILITY

Pride makes us artificial, and humility makes us real.
-Thomas Merton

Having humility is freedom from pride or arrogance. The quality or state of being humble is to accept the honor of what's morality.

My humble journey

My humble journey has always been uncomfortable, especially when I had humble fly swatters around me at all times (the company you keep is important. I will explain this further in Chapter 6 Strong community). Growing up, I had to overcome many obstacles, but Ruby made my life livable. Ruby Lee Irons was the greatest gift God gifted me. My great-grandmother embodied the very definition of humility from head to toe. Around the age of 14, I moved in with Ruby, and what I didn't know was that I had just enrolled in Humility 101(Along with Wisdom 305, English 400, Clean Up-Master Class). Being teachable is a massive part of being able to have humility, and now that I think about it, it's funny that God would place me with an English teacher to live with throughout my most impressionable years. A person who invites the opportunity to read, invite feedback and ask relevant questions is humble. I had to become intentional in being a student at all times. This opportunity meant that I needed to be observant, attentive, and mindful of the things she would show me throughout our daily lives while living together.

I had to succumb to watching people treat my grandma like dirt, and often she would bless them and carry on with her day. Sometimes we would catch a glimpse of her flesh. This was very rare, yet hilarious. She would say things like, *"You ain't going to piss on me and call it Rainwater!"* For those who need help understanding that, she was basically saying, you're not going to lie to my face and think I don't know it's a lie. I got to experience many first-hand people use and abuse her kindness, and when she didn't return what they were giving out, they would separate themselves from her. The truth can do that to you, and she was the TRUTH! Whenever these people would come crawling back, she was just as welcoming as if they had never done anything before. It was hard to watch at times because, anyone that loves their grandma, you don't want anyone crapping all over your grandma. I will admit that it was also a struggle because her heart was so big, and I had to share it with many people. You might wonder, well, why was that hard for you? I had no desire to share my great-grandmother. Luckily, that wasn't my choice because these things were necessary for me to endure and experience. It sometimes felt like she wasn't real. I often said, *"My God, how can you continue being so humble all the time?"* It was like she was made for this, and to be honest, I wanted to be like her. Being able to acquire humility made the rest of these characteristics and tools easy to obtain and hold on to. During these lessons, I had no idea that the value of these lessons would only increase later in life.

The Ways to Find Humility

There are a lot of ways to display your humility. Most of the time, your humility only stands out when adversity comes knocking at your door. Around 12 years ago, a relative and I fell out, and to be honest, I'm not sure what initiated it. I know what kept it growing—the lack of humility that I displayed, along with a few other things. Sis, it was me. One important lesson my grandmother taught me was that humility wasn't optional, and it wasn't something that needed to be activated daily. My humility required me to be ON at all times, not just when I felt like it. When you finally embrace humility, it permits you to own up to your crap. *"Hey, I'm not perfect. I do mess up."*

It allows correction to happen without pride or ego getting in the way. Making a conscious decision about what is more important…your ego and pride or your healing? It's easy to allow your ego to hop in the driver's seat and uber you somewhere you don't want to be. Humility allows you to open up opportunities to be better and not revisiting familiar, complicated places anymore. I was listening to a TD Jakes' sermon, and he stated that when we listen intentionally and give our undivided attention, we can avoid confusion and chaos. Don't be more concerned about your pride than your productivity. Humility is an inner awareness of your fragility. I will give you some examples of how to demonstrate humility.

11 TIPS

Here are some tips on practicing humility.

01 Listen to others

02 Practice Mindfulness

03  Be Grateful

04 Ask For Help

05 Seek Feedback From Wise Counsel

06  Service Others

07 Admit When When You're Wrong

08  Don't Worry About Getting The Credit

09 Do The Right Thing

10  Let God Direct Your Thinking

11 Exercise Your Spirit

Practice mindfulness

Mindfulness is the quality or state of being conscious or aware of something. Focus on the present. Look at the trees—the grass and listen to the wind. Where are you right now? Be grateful for what you have. I often hear other relatives mention pictures or conversations that they have gotten to experience with the relative I was currently estranged from. So, with my inquiring mind, I decided that I wanted to check out their excursions for myself. I was on social media one day, and I got the urge to check out my relative's page. As I get on the page, I immediately see all the beautiful places everyone had been referring to. My relative had been all over the world during the years of us not speaking. Immediately, I got a rush of unexpected emotions. My first feeling was regret. I thought about the recent tragic passing of Nipsey Hussle, and my heart sank. I felt that I never wanted to miss out on experiencing someone that I genuinely love, just because I allowed confusion, pride, and ego to dictate our future. I knew then that only I have the power to stop this from happening.

Mindfulness is about these three components.

● **Intention** –Your purpose is what you hope to get.

I had decided that I wanted to reconcile this relationship. I knew I needed to go into this without any expectations. I just wanted that person to know that I was present and willing to move forward and was open to any suggestions they may have had.

● **Attention** –Paying attention to your inner or outer **mindfulness** experiences.

I focused on enjoying her pictures and things that she was open to sharing with the world. I was interested in where she had been and where she was going because I also love exploring the world. I was interested in wanting them to know that I loved them deeply and I truly missed them.

● **Attitude** – paying attention to **mindfulness** within individual perspectives, such as curiosity, acceptance, and kindness.

I had re-positioned my heart to be acceptant and kind. My goal was to create a new beginning. I figured that anyone that loved discovery would be open to discovering new depths of our relationship.

Understanding the 3 States of mind

Ask yourself these following questions:

Emotional Mind

The state of mind where we feel the depth of our emotion and act from an emotional state can be described as an emotional mind. In extreme cases, one can react impulsively out of anger without thinking about the consequences. This part responds to feelings, even if those feelings don't match what we observe.

**Give an example of emotional mind this week
(Please describe your emotions ? Your Thoughts? Your behaviors?)**

Reasonable Mind

The reasonable mind is the logical state of mind that people use when doing math, reading a map, and various other concrete tasks.

**Give an example of reasonable mind this week
(Please describe your emotions ? Your Thoughts? Your behaviors?)**

Wise Mind

A wise mind is in the middle of both a logical and emotional mind. Wise minds are aware of their feelings, and they decide how to honor their feelings and goals. If angered, they would acknowledge their feelings and act in a way that would not negatively affect them.

**Give me an example of wise mind this week
(Please describe your emotions ? Your Thoughts? Your behaviors?)**

Mindfulness
3 States of mind.

Let's observe ourselves in 3 states of mind.
Place in the right space things that are going on in your mind. Start with writing down how you feel, next write down what you think, and then use your wise mind to balance your emotions and logic to make a wise decision.

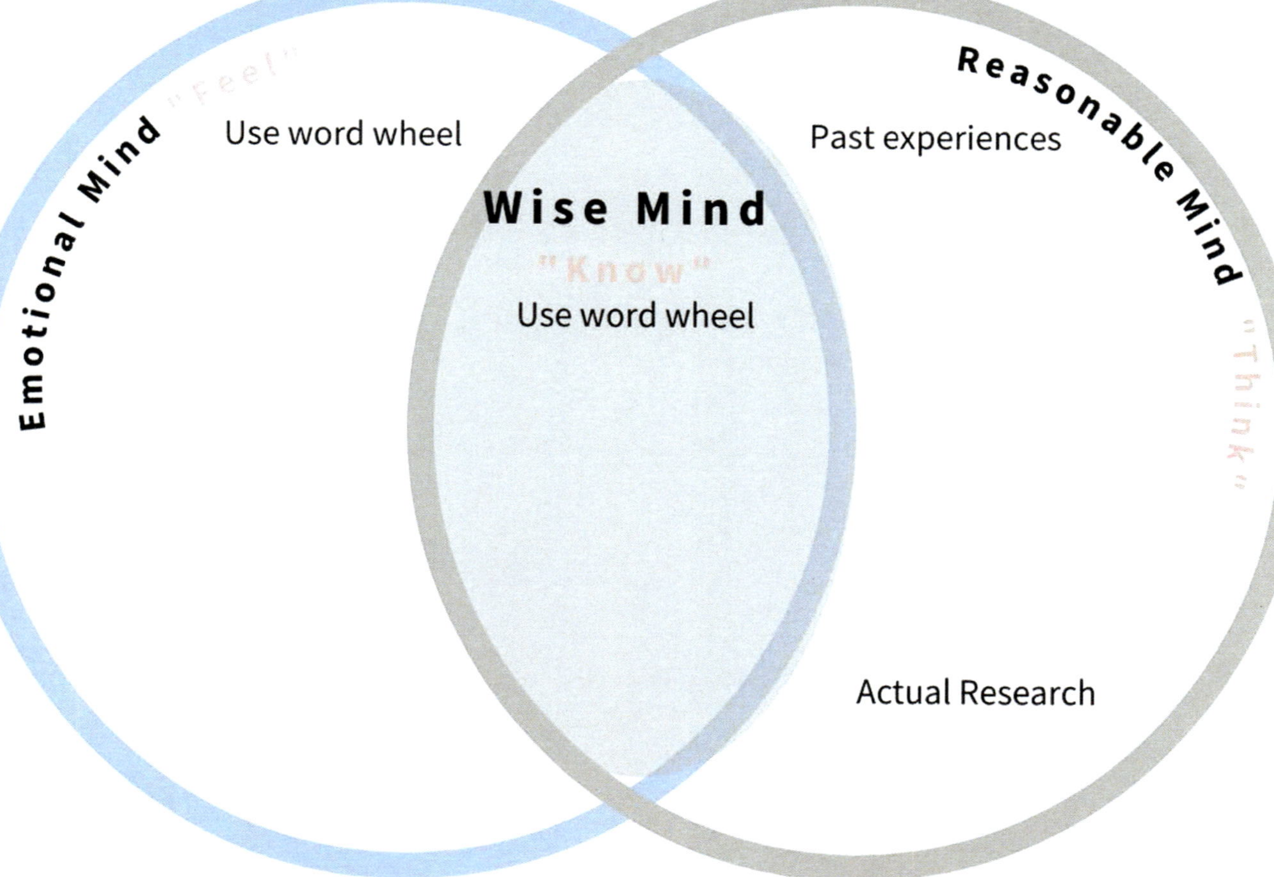

Mindfulness Body Scan

The body scan can be performed while lying down, sitting, or in other postures. The steps below are a guided meditation designed to be done while sitting.

Ask for help

When you need help, please don't be so proud that you allow yourself to endure more trials and tribulations than intended for you. Part of being humble is knowing we are here to do things with one another. I was not going to go into this situation alone. The reason is because all the other times I had approached this with the same mindset. This may have led me to where we were at in the beginning. It was time to humble myself and recognize that two are better than one.

Two are better than one,
because they have a good return for their labor:
If either of them falls down,
one can help the other up.
But pity anyone who falls
and has no one to help them up.
Also, if two lie down together, they will keep warm.
But how can one keep warm alone?
Though one may be overpowered,
two can defend themselves.
A cord of three strands is not quickly broken.
Ecclesiastes 4:9-12

Spend time listening to others

Often, we don't realize the importance of getting guidance and wisdom from others. If you struggle with this, it is possible because it causes us to doubt our own beliefs. It was time to seek feedback from my wise counsel (We will discuss that more in Chapter 6). Did you know that you could avoid a lot of mistakes if you just asked for help? I reached out to a few members of my strong community to get some advice on my future intentions with this family member. The feedback I received was a mixture of good and bad which I expected to be quite honest. The excellent feedback focused on my intentions and what I ultimately wanted from this reconciliation. The not-so-good feedback remained focused on things that I had no control over, which was the PAST. As I absorbed what each person said, I needed to have one more critical conversation with God. In this conversation, I wanted to do less talking and more listening to what He had to say, and boy, was it a mouthful. He allowed me to see things that I had been blind to during our previous years of discourse between them and myself. This talk gave me perspective from God's eye.

Perspective- is the way you see something.

The word *perspective* originates from the word optics, which means to see through. God's perspective allowed me to see through the situation. For years, I had just been looking at the disconnect for what it simply was, a disconnect. God allowed me to see right through it. Humility wrapped from head to toe. Yep, you guessed it. Those valuable lessons Ruby Lee taught me early on were now funneling out the flood gates, and I was in for a big splash. My great grandmother's biggest test of humility was with people in our family. She made sure that she always mimicked Jesus' grace and mercy no matter what. The one thing I can remember my grandmother saying to me was that there was always more to the story, and most likely, I didn't have it all, so who was I to make a judgment on my own?

The way of a fool is right in his own eyes,
but a wise man listens to advice.
-Proverbs 12:15

If you already struggle with change, this can also heighten your fear of uncertainty. Your relationship with God is instrumental during this process because, in these moments, you can pray for discernment to help you filter out what's real and what's hot air when listening to others.

Where there is no guidance, people fall,
but in an abundance of counselors, there is safety.
-Proverbs 11:14

Asking Questions

Asking questions is essential for clarifying information and understanding things. **Ask yourself these 3 questions when inquiring about something before making a hasty decision.**

WHAT DO YOU KNOW

I'm toxic

WHAT DO YOU WANT TO LEARN

Where and how to remove them

WHAT YOU LEARNED

Reading this book and doing the worksheets will help me

Service others

To serve others means to give someone service or to present someone with something. When you begin to do things to serve others and not yourself, you fill yourself with purpose and gratitude. Servicing others can come in many forms, and I have experienced many of them. There would be times where I may have given my time for free or anything that could help someone. On this day, my service was to restore brokenness in my family.

My relative had just posted the picture of a lifetime. Versailles was the post that got me. I was in awe, and I commented on their Facebook story. That comment initiated the fitting of my humility armor.

The comment read: "This is one of my dreams to go here. This is so dope. This is so dope!"

On September 13th, 2019, this relative had decided to reply, and their reply was pleasant. It came with a bit more than what I had prepared for myself.

*The text read, **relative**: "It was breathtaking. You definitely should go. I'm not going to front or sweep things under the rug as if things never happened, as some tend to do. For us to even begin to be cordial, I'm going to need an apology."*

As you read above, I had no idea why or what I had done to this person, and I felt for a brief moment shock. *"Are you kidding me?"* I said to myself.

They owed me an apology. That feeling quickly dissipated. I realized that my purpose was to initiate some reconciliation or at least see where I stood. It wasn't my job to get offended. Stay focused, Tiffynee.

I have witnessed people in the midst of servicing someone allow an offense to come in and determine that they will no longer be servicing that person. Stay focused!

Admit when you are wrong

Admit when you're wrong, promptly! Yes, I know this can be pretty hard to do, primarily when you feed off of being right. Let me let you in on a little secret: I'd rather be wrong to one than a thousand people. When you allow yourself to settle in the idea that you're not wrong, you become infected. You take that infection and pass it on to others (i.e., your children). The quicker you learn to admit when you are wrong, the more opportunity for evolving takes off. I choose to grow every day!

Own up to your shit. It shows that you are not arrogant or prideful and can make mistakes and live to see another day. Showing yourself mercy and grace proves that you're human. Arrogance destroys your opportunity to grow. Humility is not a facial expression, so don't buy into the facade of humility. Don't be overly impressed by who looks humble. My relative messaged me back and spoke about the things that she needed me to address.

Realistically, I had a few choices, but to be honest, I only wanted to adhere to one option: to hear her out and respect her for what I caused her to experience. During this time, I had a lot of things that were happening to me emotionally.

Did you know that you can't tell someone what they experienced? If they experienced that, it is valid for them. I can tell people what my intent was, but I don't know how to make them feel about it. I could hear my grandmother speaking to me, instructing me to say things and allowing myself to listen to what my relative was saying. What I was experiencing was beyond surreal. All of a sudden, I felt a massive rush of emotions surround me, and I could not escape it. I was hysterically crying while trying to hide it from my husband on his birthday. I was trying to grasp why I was crying, and it honestly felt like I could feel all of that person's hurt. I didn't appreciate how that made me feel.

Bring Forth Your Best Self

Let's bring forth our best selves, and to do that, we will need to make some changes to the habits that hinder us from moving forward.

Answers these 4 questions.

HABITS I WOULD LIKE TO KEEP

kindness towards others

HABITS YOU WANT TO CHANGE

judging others

BEHAVIORS I WOULD LIKE TO KEEP

saying I love you even when I'm angry

BEHAVIORS I NEED TO CHANGE

cussing so quickly before gaining my composure

__Ask God to direct your thinking.__

This task requires you to practice spiritual exercises. Now, I don't routinely physically exercise (as I should), but this type of training involves what we talked about in chapter two—going to God and your mentors, clarifying things, and feeding your mind with good fruit. I needed to gather myself because I was seriously talking myself out of what I was being directed to do. I needed to sit and be quiet for a few moments because I was feeling weird. As I was listening, the same things started coming through, and at this point, I thought I was going crazy. So, I texted my best friend. Here was our exchange

ME: *"It's funny how much emotion we as people attach to an apology. I can't believe that this entire time that we haven't been talking that all it was going to take was an apology. When I got their reply this morning, I was going to screenshot it and ask you what you think. Then I quickly remembered that I don't need you to tell me to apologize. If it means healing someone, I'll apologize to whoever wants an apology."*

ME: *"Some will question did she deserve an apology, and I would answer that does anyone deserve an apology? If an apology is what they require to move past anything that could be potentially holding them back from greatness."*

ME*: "An apology is what they will get."*

ME: *"As one of my true friends, I asked you never to allow me to block my blessings over an apology. Please remind me of what there is all to gain and for me to remember that this is bigger than me."*

My Bestie: Blackheart emoji x 3 and Handclap (iPhone)

I offered up a video apology as well because I needed them to see it in my eyes that I was genuine and sincere. I was exhausted from carrying the weight of us not speaking, and God had directed me to unpack the load.

Be honest

Being honest is a challenging task for most. In the video, I spoke of my true feelings and what my heart desired, which was reconciliation, love, and union. That was all I could get out. Speaking from my heart, I feel, I allowed my relative to get a glimpse into my world and see where my heart was. A text message saying I'm sorry is one thing, but someone getting to look into your eyes, which are the windows to your soul, allows someone a better perspective of where you stand truthfully. During this exchange, after receiving the video, it was then expressed to me that my apology was then genuinely accepted. They, too, had been contemplating how they could reply to me (needing to bring attention to some things that were a requirement for them to move forward).

When you discover your self-revelation, you will be so attracted to the truth that a lie gives you an allergic reaction. Well, it does for me. Keep Benadryl on deck while you work this thing out!

Show gratitude

Being grateful is one of my most prized possessions. I can't even describe the amount of gratitude I had after this exchange. I just knew that I was highly thankful to all the lessons Ruby had taught me. That same day I posted a meme that read: *God is working out things you haven't even prayed for.* I was thankful for many reasons but here are just a few:

- I got the urge that day to check out their page.
- That they visited a place, I was dreaming about.
- That I dared even to comment and not just be a ghost watcher (Yes, we see all of you).
- That it took her a few weeks to reply- we often rush things and then ruin them before they can even bloom.
- That Ruby Lee had taught me the fundamentals of humility.
- Reconciliation.
- Love.

My gratitude supersedes everything because it is an honor to be blessed. Humility is working on your appreciation. I sometimes sit back and reflect on all that I have been through. Knowing how many times my life swung past the death angel's face. I can only be grateful.

Grateful Web

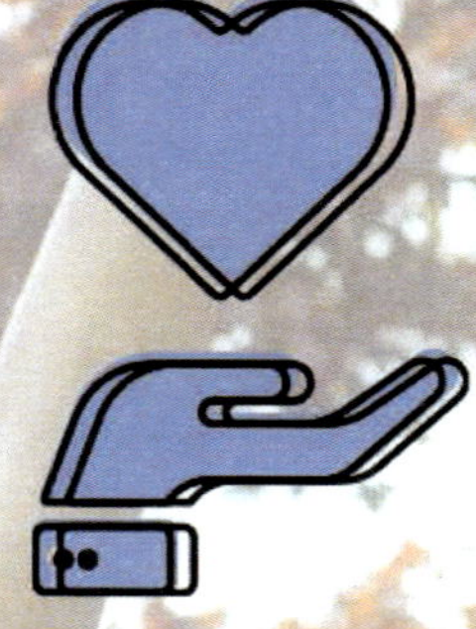

Make the web connect to all the things that you are grateful for.
Fill in all the blank circles with things that you're grateful for.

I Am Grateful For

Don't be worried about who receives credit.

Who cares who gets the credit? Please remind yourself that credit only lasts a moment. It is the least important outcome. We tend to think that if someone knows who is responsible for a good deed, we get box seats in heaven. Well, I haven't visited heaven yet, but I'm skeptical that you're going to get any recognition on things that you are supposed to be doing. If you know families, there is always someone that notices you and that person are talking again, and they need all the details because this story must be juicy, right? You need to decide the intent of your good deed in the first place. Was it to receive recognition or to solve a problem? When you realize what the answer is, capture it because this is the current state of where your heart is. I decided that this wasn't about me and that something more significant was to come out of this. I chose not to divulge the details, but to delight in the fact that we are working on a healthier relationship.

Do the right thing all the time

Do the right thing all the time, especially when no one is looking. Yo, someone is always looking (GOD). Most of the time, someone else sees you doing it too. Ask yourself an honest question. If you were to see a movie about your life story, what do these moments look like? I will not tell any lies. Some things were sent to distract me from being focused on our healing during this transition. Such as side conversations led by folks who couldn't get over the fact that you apologized or that this thing is really over between you and them. Please pay attention to the folks that hang on to yesterday longer than you do. Get rid of them folks—but recognize that it would be up to me to choose whether I will allow myself to be derailed or intentional about my objective and do the right thing. I DID THE RIGHT THING! Sometimes I cringe when I think back on some of the stupid *ish* I did. In the past, I was the person who would toss something in the garbage can and watch it not make it in and walk away. Welp, the conviction I get to pick that crap up is so intense now that I can't just leave something laying there. Triggered Anyone? PICK UP YOUR ISH.

Root for everyone to win

In the words of Issa Rae, *"I am rooting for everyone Black."* I want everyone to win. My goal is to encourage whomever I encounter to be great and the best version of themselves. If you can find any research or evidence that states that doing something like this subtracts value from you, let me know how that works out for you. When you have this type of mindset, I promise you nothing will get in your way. You will have people that will say that if they don't support you, don't support them. That's the wildest thing I have ever heard when the same person will say that they are the epitome of humility. Check your heart. If it takes their support for you to support them, your support was never genuine.

It was conditional. I had missed out on so many years of that person's travels and posts. I make sure I see, like, and sometimes comment on the exciting things they share. I had always had a love for the free-spirited life they live, and that shouldn't change now!

"Disguise uncertainty with arrogance, and you lose the opportunity for revelation, which makes you stuck on your journey."

-TD JAKES

Self Examination Tracker

It's important to reflect on yourself. This worksheet helps you become aware of what you're doing well with and what areas you need to work on. Use this journal to track your progress practicing healthier behaviors.

Date	WHAT EVENT TRIGGERED THE BEHAVIOR	Are you happy with the outcome?	What do you wish you did better to handle this situation?	What will you be mindful of to change in your behavior the next time?
5/5/21	Peer pressure to drink	No	not have drank so much	to either manage my liquor intake or manage my emotions prior

GOD'S PROMISE

Humility
The reward for humility and fear
of the Lord is riches and honor
and life.

Proverbs 22:4 ESV

THE TIFFANATOR

Talk to God

This is one of the easiest things to do because it's just like journaling but with a purpose and person in mind.

CHAPTER 5

THE SHOVEL - HAVE COURAGE

Grab your shovel. It's time to dig this *ish* up. It is essential that you have the right type of digging tool for the kind of ground you will be digging in. This tool will make it easy for you to dig deep holes with the smallest diameter necessary to remove your targets. It's going to take courage to dig up the old you and the toxic parts of you. Most of the time, we want to ignore the ugly details. A part of our discovery is to acknowledge who we are and welcome who we are chosen to be. It won't always be a pretty sight to see, and it will take a lot of strength to complete this process. So, gear up and grab a good shovel.

> *"Be of good courage, and let us be courageous for our people, and the cities of our God, and may the Lord do what seems good to him." "But you, take courage! Do not let your hands be weak, for your work shall be rewarded." "Wait for the Lord; be strong, and let your heart take courage; wait for the Lord!*
>
> *-2 Samuel 10:12*

The best way to find success in life is to live a courageous life. We can't allow fear to dictate our decisions. Courage isn't something you're just born with. It's a quality that we can deliberately develop. People often think of courage in terms of physical bravery, risking our lives to save a person's life if it is in danger. It takes courage to talk to new people, stand up for our beliefs, start a business, find a new career path, find a permanent change of scenery, and write a freaking book. In any situation, big or small, it's a quality we use. The tiniest bit of fear and risk still exists even, and these come up nearly every day. Sis, be courageous.

The not so Fearless Woman

Those who know me might assume that I'm courageous as they come. I mean…look, I wrote a book. Look here world, your girl be scared, lol. Some of my greatest fears have prevented me from being the best version of myself. My fears feel so big and scary. By the time I have sorted through them, they are so small that it's embarrassing to admit that I was afraid. It reminds me of this time I saw this spider on the ground in our house. I took off running and screaming. My daughter, Jai, who was around four at the time, said to me, *"Who is bigger, you or the spider?"* I just looked at her, dumbfounded and riddled with a slight sense of stupidity. It was I who was bigger. I'm telling you it be your own kids. Small fears can be just as debilitating as big ones. As a mother, I struggle with the constant anxiety of something happening to my children. At one point, it got so bad that I wasn't letting them go many places. One day, I happened to be talking to my aunt, and she revealed to me that she too struggled with those thoughts. After walking me through her similar fear, she told me that she wanted to gift me something to help along my journey. She gave me a bat to knock down fear's doors. She walked me through this process I like to call, *Deconstructing the Fear Wall.*

Fear Steps

Start by writing down the fears that you are facing on each step on the staircase. This gives head start to turn the lights on your fears.

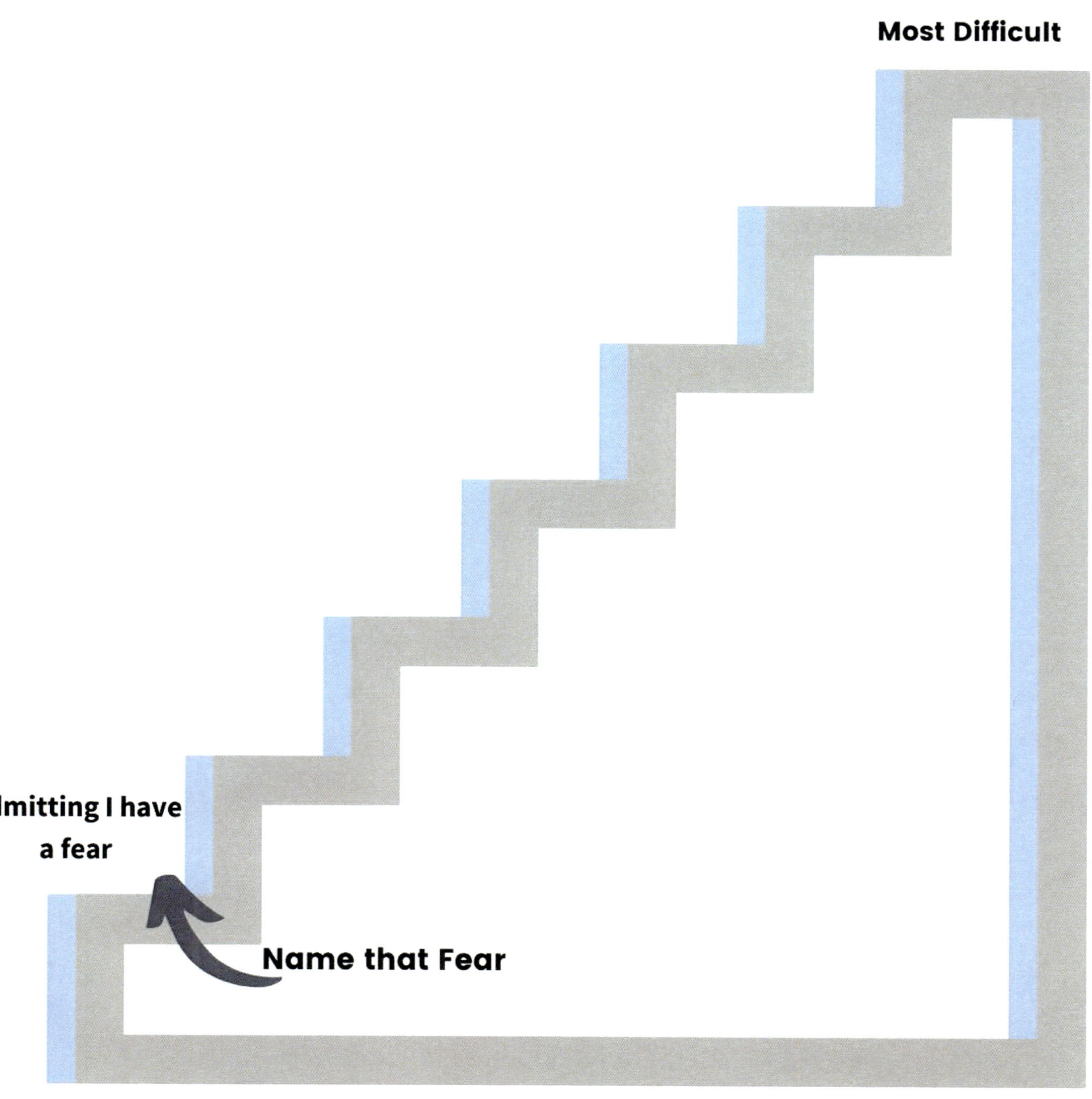

Turn on the lights

She said that it was necessary to express my fear out loud because that would shed light on the darkness of my fear. When something is hidden, it can manifest into things that are not healthy for you. I'll even give you a better example: Roaches roam in the dark. When the lights come on they scatter. When I don't acknowledge that I have them, I allow my fears to grow and manifest. Turn the lights on.

Locate your fear

She said, once the light is on, locate your fear to see where it is. The fear of something happening to my children derived from near-death experiences they encountered coming into this world. When I was pregnant with both of my girls, I was considered High Risk with a lot of medical conditions that could possibly be carried on to one of my girls. My oldest was born 4lbs, 3oz and had to stay in the NICU for a bit. My youngest was born early as well, but she had a few complications as well. The thought of me not being able to protect them or save them crippled me. After acknowledging where the fear had originated from, it was easier to throw logic against it.

Detach them from reality

She instructed me to separate my fears from the thoughts of "what if". If I allow my children to go outside and not watch them, someone could take them. That was my thought process. The reality of that is I don't let my children go out without someone that I trust keeping a good eye on them. Tearing down your fears becomes easier when you apply logic to them. Just like who is bigger, the spider or you? Once I was able to complete that effectively, I could kick the fear wall down.

Have an Inner Hype-Man

I have a little mantra as well.

"That can't happen. It won't happen. I won't let it happen, so TRY AGAIN."

It took a large amount of courage to kick that fear down, but the reward of not having to deal with it was more significant than being scared.

Myths For Vulnerability

Myth	Truth
Vulnerbility is a weakness.	Vulnerability is the most accurate measure of courage.
I can opt of out vulnerability.	If you allow vulnerability to hide, it will seek you out!
Vulnerbility is oversharing.	Vulnerability requires us to share our feelings and experiences with people who have earned the right to hear them, this requires trust and boundaries.
I can go at vulnerbility alone.	We are wired to have a connection with others.

Embrace Vulnerability

I'm able to maintain my courage because I have acquired characteristics and qualities to help me. To be vulnerable means to be at risk of experiencing harm. Vulnerability is the core of all emotions and feelings. To feel and express honestly is to be vulnerable. To believe vulnerability is a weakness is to think that the ability to feel is weak. News flash: you get up every day and feel. Sis, let me tell you something. You are strong.

In February 2020, about five days after my birthday, I had another death scare. Did I say another? Oh yes, indeed. From a Dr's perspective, the person writing this book right now isn't supposed to be here. I SHOULD BE DEAD!

In 2010, I was diagnosed with congestive heart failure. My heart was functioning at 14%, and I was told, verbatim, by the attending doctor, "YOU ARE GOING TO DIE."

Hearing those words in conjunction with being sick for three months prior, feeling that life was ending soon, I really can't explain what I was experiencing besides pure fear. As the doctor spouted those words out, immediately, tears began to fall from my face. I knew this was it. I was leaving a three-year-old motherless and all I could do was cry. When would people ask her, *"How is your mother?"* Her exact words to people would be *"All she does is cry, cry, cry, sleep and cry some more."*

Well, for the .03 seconds that my older sister, Shontee, allowed me to cry, she turned to me and said, *"Shut up those tears, and wasting your energy on crying. We need to use that energy to fight this."*

I felt hopeless. Life was just dangling in front of me.

All I knew was, in that moment, someone from my strong community was holding me up because I didn't have it in me. The past two months, I had consistently vomited all day, every day. I experienced severe cardiac asthma, which resulted in having zero energy to do anything. I was empty. If anyone had an outing scheduled or planned, it required me to get fully dressed, hair included, taking a minimum three-hour to complete. I would have to rest in 3-4 min intervals. When they had discovered the CHF, my heart had doubled twice its size. About 15 lbs. of fluid was surrounding my heart. My heart was telling us that it had enough. We will get into the full story in book number two, but for right now, let me tell you where my vulnerability finally came in. For most that know me, this isn't a story I share much because most people use it as a weapon of either destruction, judgment, or fear. To be honest, I don't have time for any of those. I'm sharing it in this book because I know the importance and the weight of it now versus when I use it freely and incautiously.

On the 25th of February,2020, almost ten years to the date when this whole tribulation began, this near-death experience felt similar to the last one. For some reason, I thought to myself, *"Death angel, you have finally caught up with me...DAMN!"*

 We believe that before Covid was confirmed to be out here, I think I had it and was suffering from the ramifications of the virus. I had arrived at day 12 of being sick for the second time in 2 months. The doctor had prescribed a few different medications to counteract my sickness. Having viral Cardiomyopathy (Which is the type of CHF I have), I'm treated a bit differently when the common cold or flu comes around. All of the perks are pulled out to protect this beautiful heart of mine. Unfortunately, two of the prescriptions decided to have beef inside my body and caused me to have an adverse reaction, which caused my heart rate to speed up to about 16o+ per min while I was resting. If you don't know what that feels like, let me tell you, it feels like a horse is running on your chest. The pounding of my heart was so rapid and hard I felt weak and faint after about 2 hours of experiencing this feeling and being in my room enduring the pain and agony alone. My husband had just recently left for work, and I was crouched over in our bedroom dying slowly. My daughter happened to come into my room. She began to interrogate me, eventually having to take matters into her own hands because I had settled in with defeat, and my pride wouldn't allow me to be too vulnerable in front of my kids. The attitude of a *strong black woman that needs no help* was ultimately going to kill me, but GOD! She called 911, and déjà vu appeared like it was 2010 all over again. As they wheeled me away on the stretcher, I couldn't help but think, *"wow, this is the last time I'm going to see my kids."* What a memory! That night my parents, husband, and children rushed themselves to the hospital because they knew what this journey looked like as well. We waited for four hours for my heart rate to finally go down. That was when we all were able to take a deep breath and relax. Well, they did. That exhale didn't happen until the next day for me.

Get Naked

Vulnerability is like getting naked. As you take off layers of yourself the self-discovery will begin.
This is what Self Intimacy looks like!
Write down below things that you want to be totally open about .....

People who live fear-based lives have little or no confidence in themselves. If you feel afraid of other people seeing who you are, you're going need to open up and become more vulnerable. This is really the only way to approach your fears once you have admitted to them. It's time to bury them.

"Blessed are those who have regard for the weak; the LORD delivers them
in times of trouble."
-Psalm 41:1 (NIV)

Grieve your weakness. Whatever your weakness is, allow yourself to experience the painful emotions necessary to heal. I consider crying to be a way to purge of all my shortcomings.

I woke up the next morning in my bed, and all I could think was, "Thank God I'm alive." I went into my office and decided that I needed to gather myself because I was a mess. I was thankful to be alive, but I was mad that I, once again, had lost the concept of God's promise for me. I cried like a baby. I mean snot and everything. I purged all of the bad thoughts I had about myself.

Don't underestimate the power of acceptance. When we accept our hurt and the truth, we can go to God with it. Can you imagine when we cry and give it to God? He collects our tears so we can start the process of healing. As I cried, I felt this sense of calmness reside over me. No one was in the room, but I felt the presence of a hug. What a warming feeling to have when you are all alone. I think that's why they tell you a close hand doesn't get fed. Open them hands up and take God's healing. Its FREE!

Please don't take it back. The triggers will come, but you must have the courage to face them with good judgment to overcome them. As I sat there, I kept feeling like something was telling me that this would happen again, just wait and see. I had to think with purpose and with good intentions not to allow this to happen again. I had to come clean I needed to tell my pride and ego that I was giving them some time off because I needed to be free of them for a while. See, your ego and your pride are like your uninvited entourage. They pop up on the scene just to be seen. At this time in my life, I didn't need to be seen. I needed to be heard.

Accept God's strength. Being vulnerable allows me to show my humility in the purest form. It gives me strength when I'm honest about my feelings and wisdom and about how I handle them. It was time for me to be intentional about being vulnerable, and I needed to accept all that God had granted me to face myself and others.

Grieve Your Weaknesses

Once you identify your weaknesses it's essential that you grieve them and walk yourself through the grieving process.
Write down below your weaknesses and grieve them through the stages.

The 7 stages of grief

- Shock and denial.
- Pain and guilt
- Anger and bargaining.
- Depression
- The upward turn
- Reconstruction and working through.
- Acceptance and hope.

Admit and be open about your fears. You have to be intentional about talking your fears down daily. Identifying what you are terrified of gives you the information you need to overcome the fears and insecurities. What I did next shocked me a bit. I turned on my video camera, and I proceeded to shoot a two minute and fifty-eight-second video of me being completely vulnerable. I sent it to my closest friends, parents, siblings, and immediate family members. Below is the transcript of the video. (In this video, I'm crying hard, and my heart is wide open. Video will be available on YouTube.)

"I think it's about time that I share this with everybody. As some of you guys know that last night, I had a near death experience, and I thought that was it for me. To be honest, I've been feeling like that for about the last past year. As I began to go through my journey of being a better person appreciating life, I just kind of felt like, I'm not going to live as long as I think I am going to. That's why it's extremely important for me to be a good person and tell everybody I love them and that I appreciate them every chance I get. Some people have a fear of dying. I don't. I just want to make sure that when I do leave, that I leave a good impression in people's hearts. It's just something that I thought was going to eventually happen to me because of all this good stuff that has been happening to me, and it honestly felt too good to be true. So, I appreciate everybody. I love everybody. I ask you just to keep me your thoughts. I'm not thinking bad thoughts or that I don't want to die or anything. I just have this feeling of death hovering over me for a long time. I think that now it's about time that I probably be honest and real about how I have been truly feeling. I'm focused on being the best person I possibly can be. So, thank you for all your thoughts, encouraging words and prayers."

Evaluate Your Fears

1. Take time out of your day to dispose of all the negative thoughts. When fear and anxiety flood your mind, it's impossible to think clearly.
2. Face your fears head-on. GAME ON, BITCHES!
3. Imagine the worst. Think about the worst that could happen to you with that fear.
4. Look at the evidence. Does this make sense, and is it even possible to happen to you?
5. Don't try to be perfect. The last perfect person left this earth long before you were born. Leave that to Him and strive to understand His struggles as well. (JESUS)

6. Visualize a positive thought- this will help you maintain the serotonin in your brain (the happiness hormone).

7. Talk about it. To God or someone with God-like discernment.

8. Cope with the risk and uncertainty. There are risks around every corner. Uncertainty lies in man's hands every day. The only person that knows the plans for our lives is GOD. So, let go of all of it and give it to God.

9. Continue to learn always. Growing is a part of evolution. Grow by continually learning and improving your skills. Take all opportunities to learn a new skill or acquire new knowledge. Read books about your industry and things outside of it. The more you know, the less risk you must take to be successful.

10. Accept Challenges. Confronting challenges and fears can deter you off course but stay focused. Instead of hiding, face what lies ahead. In many cases, fear is just in your head. Most of what you fear will never come to pass. Get to living and don't worry about the things that are out of your control.

Dear Friends/Family,

Being vulnerable is something that I'm usually ok with except when it comes to my health. I do not know why you ask because I have accepted that everyone lives and everyone dies (Says, Jordyn, my 8-year-old). I honestly couldn't tell you exactly what it is. I can say that being sick the majority of your life begins to take a toll on you. Mentally- for me because I hate to be a burden to anyone. It doesn't sound very good when you say it out loud, but it's a real feeling for me. After all the hospital scares and health flare-ups, I have learned to manage it within myself. I usually do not share exactly how badly I feel until it gets to the point like last night. Transparency moment:

I was sure last night I was done. I was extremely sad but happy because I honestly have turned my entire life around. I'm so glad and overly grateful for anything and everything that life has given me. What frustrates me is I have adapted myself to being very discreet when it comes to my health which you all have made a point to let me know that also. I also believe that, unfortunately, I'm not the only one.

I'm saddened that society has created a lifestyle choice for us where we honestly don't get to say, "Hey, I'm done for the day." We go until we can't go anymore.

Do I think I push myself too hard? Sometimes, but I know that I'm struggling to ask for help when I'm sick. I think part of me does not want to leave that lasting impression on my closest friends and family. (But also, not wanting to be the person where out of all the things God has encapsulated in me, people only see the girl that's sick.)

I don't have any answers today, but I know I needed to share this because, who knows maybe I could be helping someone else out.

Love,

Tiffynee Renee

Expressing this to them set me free as a person. I released myself from things that I didn't choose. Speak up and tell your truth! As I said above, this is something that you must acquire. Once it's yours, the more courageous you will become.

Deconstruct Your Fears?

De-catastrophizing means addressing these distortions.
Questions to ask might include: "Realistically, what is the worst that could happen?" and "How would I cope if the worst did happen?".
This worksheet can be used to guide a client through this de-catastrophizing process.

Worst Case Scenario

Fears can be eliminated quickly if you apply logic to them it.
This worksheet can be used to guide you to apply logic to your fear.

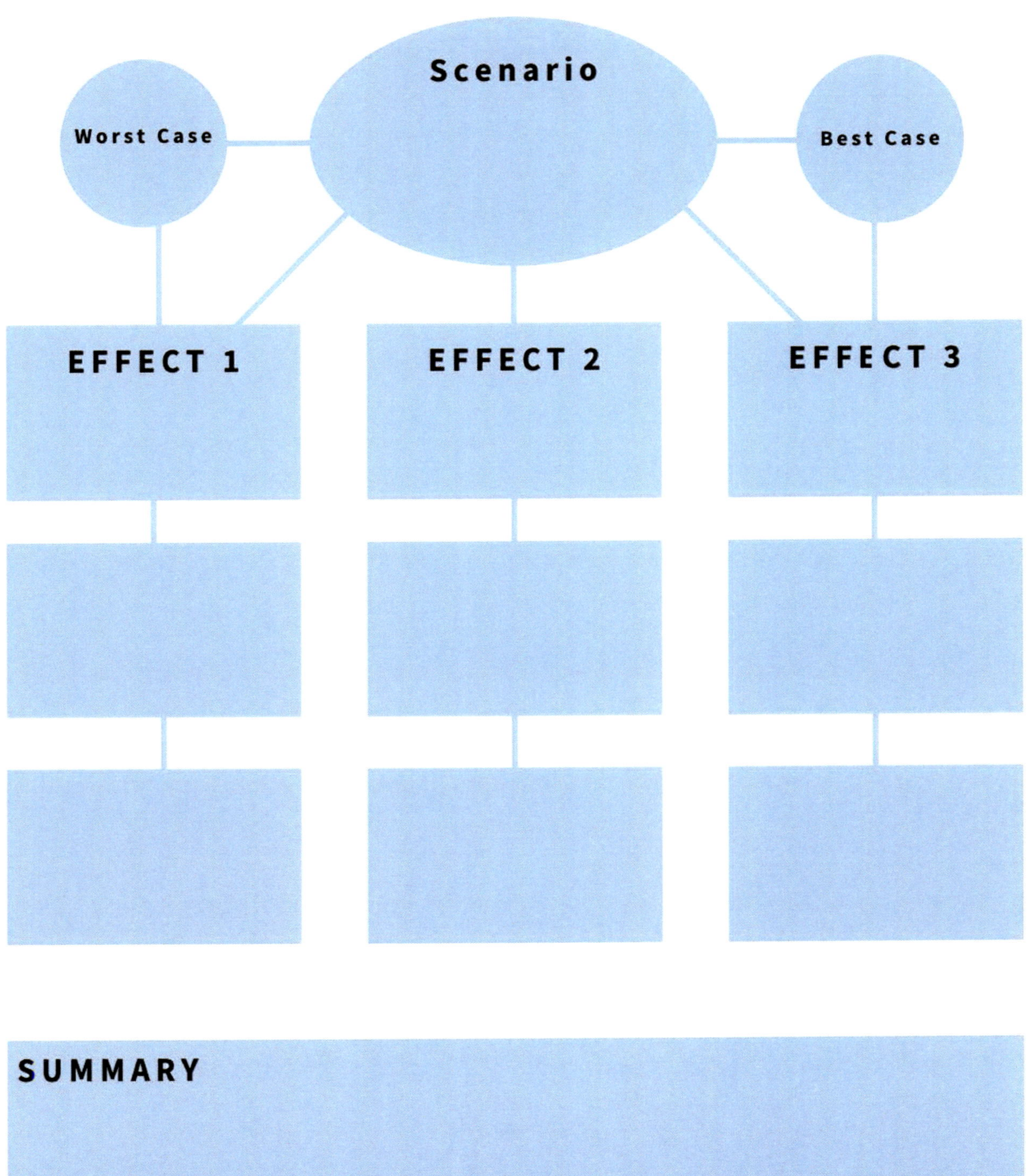

GOD'S PROMISE

Courage

Be strong and courageous. Do not be afraid or terrified because of them, for the Lord your God goes with you; he will never leave you nor forsake you.

Deuteronomy 31:6 Niv

THE TIFFANATOR

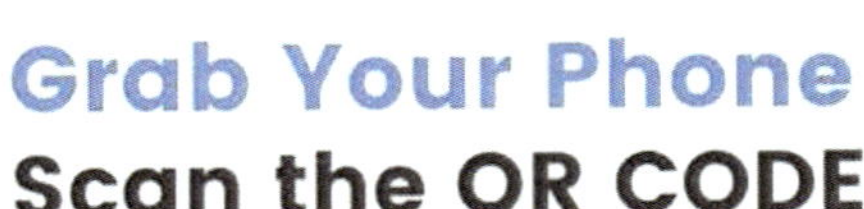

Talk to God

This is one of the easiest things to do because it's just like journaling but with a purpose and person in mind.

Chapter 6
The Sifter- Be a Part of a Strong Community

The basic idea is to sift the **soil** through a screen as much as you **would** sift ingredients for baking. **Sifting** "cleans" the **dirt**, removing large organic objects such as rocks and debris like broken glass. During this process, what is left in the sifter are things we need to take out of our soil, examine, and deal with and dispose of properly. We have a bag that we will inherit in the next chapter, but for now, you will place these items to the side as we locate them. Our strong community represents our sifter. These people are here to help us weed out the things we are too weak to do. Don't feel bad. We all need help with something.

"Listen to advice and accept discipline, and at the end, you will be counted

among the wise."

-Proverbs 19:20

Being a part of a strong community is a powerful way to keep yourself aligned with your purpose in life. Since the beginning of time, humans have formed communities so they can feel a part of something. Now, be very aware that you are the result of the people around you. So, depending on who you allow to be a part of your community will determine if you add or subtract from your life's value. Choosing the people that you're going to let in your community requires you to be fully aware of any potential effects it could have on your destiny. The goal is to surround yourself with people that align with your core values. This could have positive views focusing on changing the world for the better.

The downfall of a weak Community

Choosing my community has always been a struggle for me. I had to pay a high price for choosing the wrong members. This, in turn, caused me to detour off my path many times. I struggled to create effective filtration systems that would enable me to seek out the right members. It wasn't until I talked to my oldest daughter that I realized how this choice ultimately affected my entire family. My daughter came to me one day and told me about her best friend drama. After she finished, I asked her if she wanted my advice. She politely declined. I was appalled for a moment and, of course, asked, *"Why?"*

Here's what she said. *"Mom, I do not trust your friendship advice. I have watched people hurt you repeatedly. Not only does it make me mad at them, but it also makes me angry at you."*

With all the humility in my heart, I replied, *"I agree!"*

She was absolutely right. I had failed at this one aspect of my life tremendously. I also told her that God was trying to teach me something. Unless I was going to be intentional about getting it, it would keep happening. I looked up at her, and I said, *"LORD, YOU HAVE MADE YOURSELF LOUD AND CLEAR!"*

He used the mouth of my 13-year-old. I'm so grateful that she is a part of my strong community. It takes humility to allow yourself not to have an age restriction on your members. Anyone can be a teacher.

"Bad company corrupts good character."

-1st Corinthians 15:33

High Price to Pay

You have $25 to build 3 of your best friends.
Place their name on a piggy bank and add the things you need from them. Remember, you only have $25 each to build them. Choose wisely!

$3	$5	$9
Ride or Die	Loves to travel	God fearing
Fits in	Loyal	Inspiring
Funny	Accountable	Integrity
Goodlooking	Low Maintenance	Understanding
	Great Listener	

$5 great listener
$20 left

Most of the time, we don't consider that you have to pay taxes on things. Take into account that these people are human and leave a slight chance for error.

Over the past three years, I have had to surrender many things, including long-term friendships, essential relationships, and other things I thought weren't suitable for me. I finally realized that I lacked boundaries. I allowed people to walk around freely in my life and not realize that they had access to all the gate codes.

Pastor Michael Todd stated in his book, *Relationship Goals*, "Boundaries are the one thing God uses to help us reach our purpose. It preserves who he made us be at our core."

Bad Company Corrupts Good Fruit!

It's time to remove the filter.
Write down what you see in yourself at this moment.

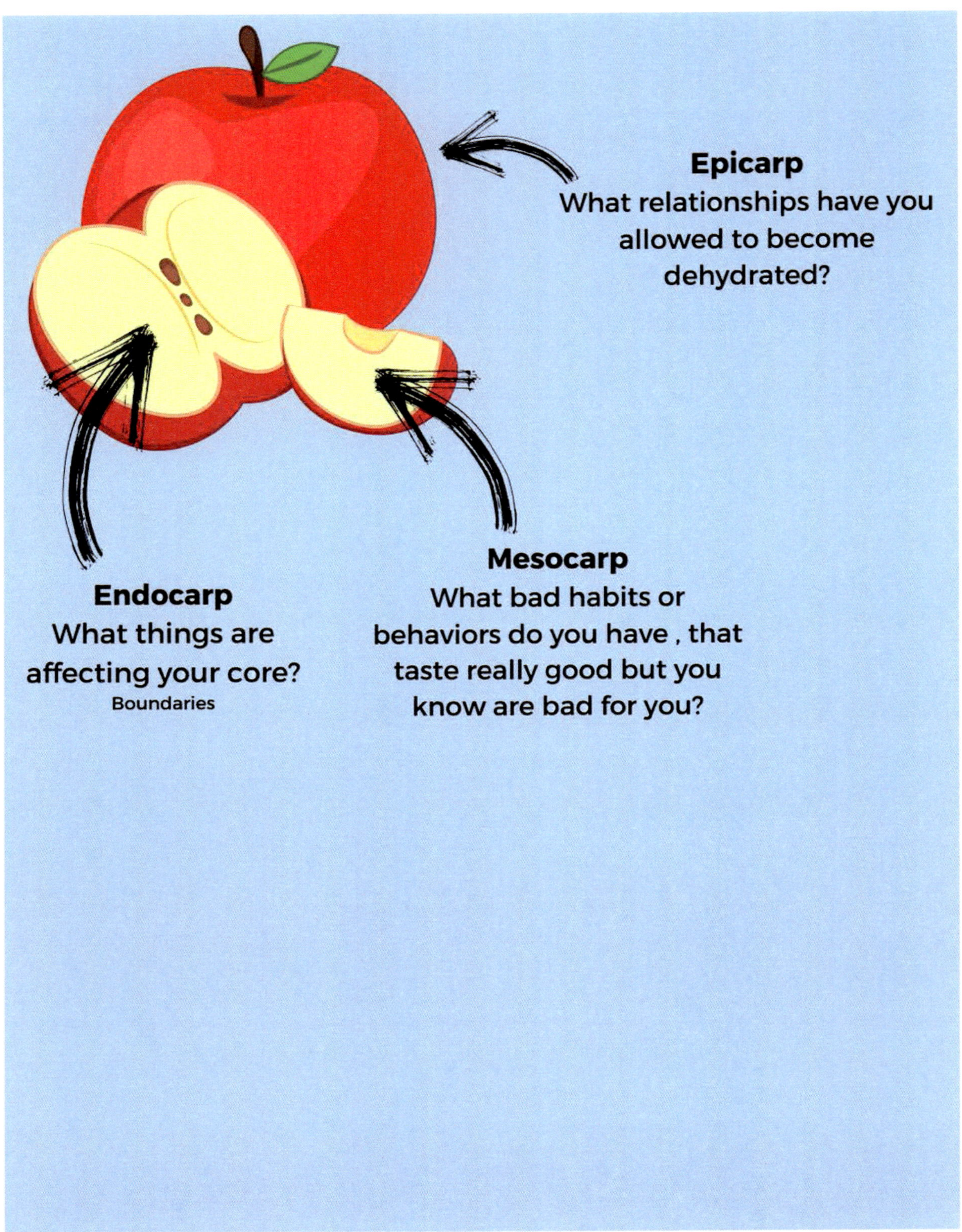

Protect your core

I asked myself, was I protecting my core? How was I guarding my heart, and did I know what that looked like for me? I had to made sure that the soil of my heart was good, but I also made sure that the people that entered my soil were good as well. Then it hit me out of nowhere. Every piece of fruit has a core, but how is it protected, and why? The core of a fruit is the central part of what contains seeds, and there are usually three layers to a piece of fruit.

1st layer (boundary) -Epicarp

The outer layer is made to be tough. We have seen many times that if you drop it or place it near a rotten piece of fruit, it can become bruised or affected by its environment.

2nd layer (boundary)- Mesocarp

The middle layer is the part that can be eaten. Your core becomes more vulnerable once the first layer is gone. There isn't much standing between your core and destruction.

3rd layer (boundary) - Endocarp

The last layer protects the seed. You're wide open at this point. Once your seed is vulnerable, you have now put God's promise at risk. We are put on this earth to be fruitful and multiply. What can you multiply if your seed is gone?

You are a fruit of the spirit, and your responsibility is to plant your seeds and produce good fruit!

Can you imagine what happens when you expose your core to the wrong people? I can. I would call it stunted growth!

I had my core all open because I lacked boundaries with all sorts of things. I needed to go through a series of questions to see what I needed to begin protecting my core.

Habits vs. Behaviors

Habits are the things a person does repeatedly until such time that it becomes automatic, they are somewhat mastered acts. While behavior is the reaction of the system to the impulses around it, habit is the thing a person does repeatedly and subconsciously until it becomes a routine.

What is affecting your core?

- Dehydrated friendships

When you leave fruit out too long, it becomes dried out. This is what some of my friendships looked like. I was allowing these people to damage my core because they were unwilling to fix theirs.

- Thirsty negative behaviors /habits.

Once you get a refrigerator, you think everything that goes into it can be preserved. Wrong! Some fruits you must treat differently. Well, I sure was treating every good or bad habit like it needed to be stored. The bad habits were just as delicious as the good ones, and they made me want more.

- No security system to guard my heart

ADT was not getting my money. My heart was unguarded and unsecured. Anyone could get in if they wanted to.

- An outdated filtration system

Tap water versus filtered water. The only thing about that luxury is making sure that your filtration system is clean and updated because if not, anything can get in, and all of it doesn't taste clean. Bad company corrupts good character.

Do you lack boundaries?

Lacking boundaries is a pretty common thing that we, as a society, suffer from. I believe that it comes from pure laziness, but it can also come from a lack of alternate solutions. Sometimes we rely on old fences built at the beginning of our relationships, aka lack of boundaries. Instead of replacing the whole fence, we board it up with old recycled pieces. Then we wonder why the same people keep affecting our core and our lives negatively in the same way. I noticed about a few dehydrated friendships that were both gradually changing, but I hadn't realized my requirements had changed to be my friend, and I was still allowing some of the same stuff to occur.

How do you put back up good boundaries?

I would suggest that you invest in a new fence. This will require people to knock or ask for permission when entering your domain. Once that fence is up, it will need you to update all access codes. This will ensure that you will not tolerate attitudes and old behaviors even if the same people get in.

I had someone say to me, *"How could you throw away 30+ years of friendship?"* I correct them and said that I didn't throw it away, I built a new fence (boundaries), and it now requires a unique access code to get in. I politely placed things that no longer aligned with my purpose outside of my old gate, re do the old one and invested in a new one. I had to raise my environmental cost.

"The biggest enemy you have in your life besides the devil and your mind is your
POTENTIAL ENVIRONMENT"
– Pastor Keion.

What does that look like for you?

This fence shouldn't be cheap, either. It should represent the things you want and need to protect in your life (Children, Partner, Mind, Soul, and Body). It will cost you. It will be worth every bit of emotional currency you have invested in being whole. The cost of peace is not affordable. You must sacrifice your old ways to inherit this lifestyle, though. My new fence is state of the art, and these access codes are only available to the ones that invest in protecting my core, a.k.a. my purpose! Yes, I'm still reading through the manual (my Bible), requesting updates through the manufacture (God), and working out all the kinks that may occur (thank God for mercy and grace).

Remember to protect your core and your mind. That what makes you sick doesn't know it makes you sick!

Build a new fence

Love your neighbor as yourself, but don't take down your fence.
-Carl Sandburg
Write down the slats healthy boundaries you need to set to build your new fence.

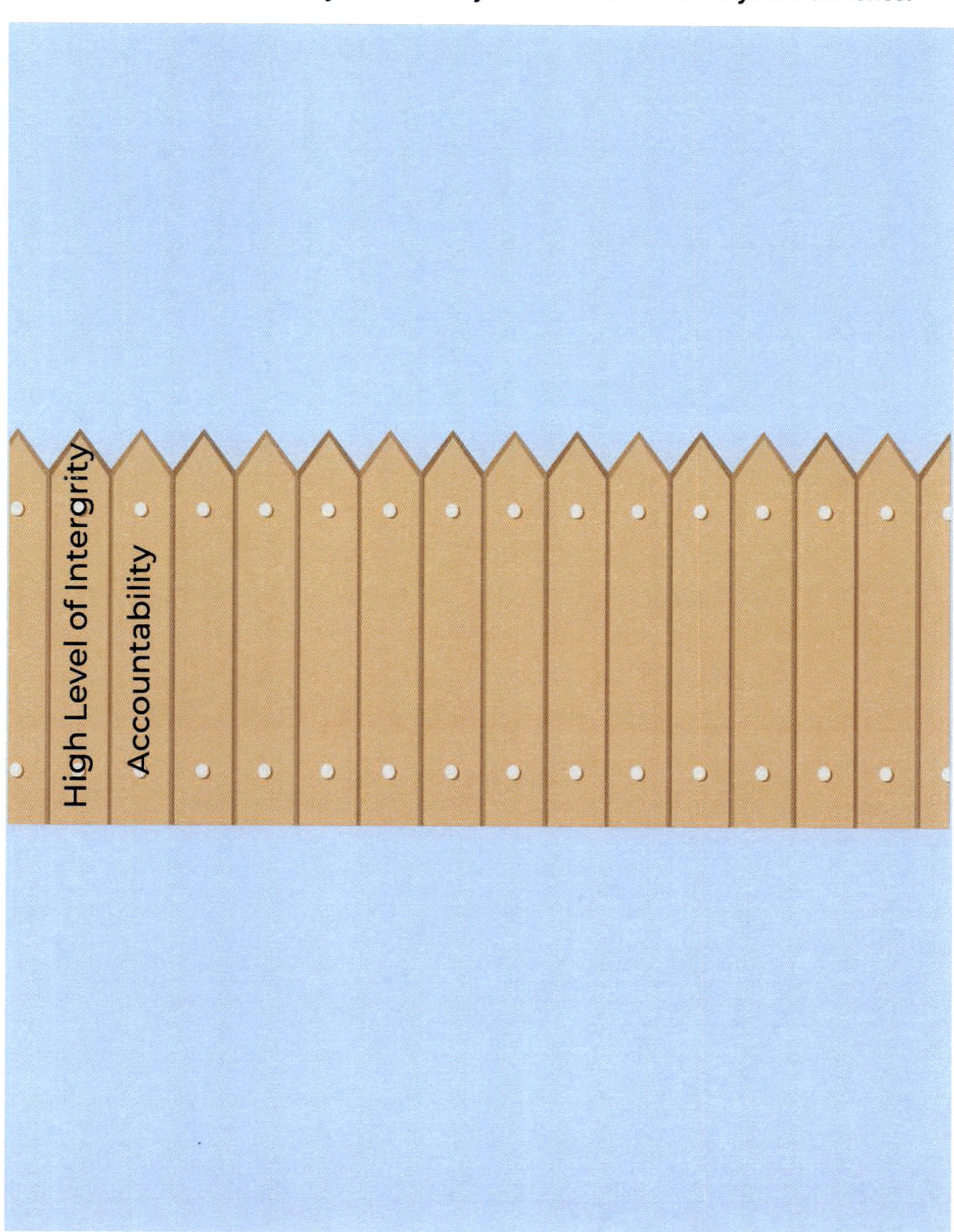

The Value of a Strong Community

Having a strong community provides you with inspiration and motivation. This type of community makes you backpedal on your negative ways of thinking about who you are and what you will be.

My branding manager, Akea, and my good Friend, Ceciela, added me to two accountability groups for entrepreneurs. If I was completely transparent, I wasn't initially interested in either because my thinking was, how can they help motivate me if they aren't doing the same as me? Well, of course, I got the exact opposite of what my negative thoughts were putting out in the atmosphere. I received an overflow of **inspiration** and **motivation** in these meetings. Every time the group's moderator would ask for folks to check-in, it was nothing, but inspiration and motivation flowing out of everyone's response. Almost everyone in the group would hype me up. So, I was always excited to share. They provided me with applause, a sense of accomplishment, and encouragement. The constructive criticism they offered was easy to take because I knew they genuinely wanted to see me win, which was what I felt for them as well. Being in those groups motivated me and inspired me to go harder and achieve bigger goals.

Being Connected

A strong community allows you to not feel alone in your failures or your successes. They offer up support to you in all your endeavors. Making mistakes is easy to do. As a matter of fact, too dang easy. We think that it's the mistake that becomes the *Pain in the ass* when the ASS (which is you) is the Pain you are sick of dealing with. Sis, it is you! You're sick of dealing with you! It isn't the mistake that keeps repeating itself. It is the person that keeps repeating the same thing expecting a different result (INSANITY). SIS, IT WAS ME!

Try reaching out to members to see if anyone has experienced your situation rather than just depending on yourself. This help could lead you to experience a valuable lesson from your mistake. This step will take vulnerability, and you have to be willing to open up to others to experience this. I quickly adapted to this skill because I'm eager to learn, and I honestly hate experiencing the same things repeatedly.

Tiff tip: ask a lot of questions for understanding because the lesson is essential to learn.

Creating Opportunity

Being a part of a strong community opens up opportunities. I know you have heard the saying, "It's not what you know, it's who you know."

I have to agree with this phrase based on my experience in these streets (streets meaning my house, lol). Based on the connections you make in life, unfortunately, your skills are not a priority to most people. The focus is placed on the people who hold the opportunity in their hands. We like to call them gatekeepers. As you start becoming a better person, your community will begin to build you up. Your opportunities will become endless. Take it from me, don't just align yourself with people you think possess the ability to open the gate for you. Let me tell you something: stepping into something like that requires a large amount of discernment and balance. If you don't have that, you will find yourself following someone else's purpose. I once became connected with a person who was my type of community partner from a bird's view. They even fit the guidelines of someone who had many opportunities to offer: a strong following, popular, talented, and much more. I failed to see that this wasn't the person God wanted to take me to the next level. That was a hard pill to swallow because this person could give me the opportunities that I thought my heart truly desired. Only to find out during a 45 day fast that God had other plans for me and my community members who were about to change drastically. My heart needed a tune-up.

*"Take delight in the Lord, and he will give you the **desires of your heart**. Commit **your** way to the Lord; trust in him, and he will do this: He will make **your** righteous reward shine like the dawn, **your** vindication like the noonday sun"*

– Psalm 37:4-6.

Do you know how easy it is to think something is a true desire of your heart, but be fooled by your heart? Yes, your heart can deceive you. Normally, it is because, like in the Map chapter, you don't know where it is so it's hard to locate.

Bring on the Fun

Being a part of a strong community also brings you a lot of fun. There are a lot ways to have fun and celebrate when you are in a strong community. As I mentioned before, one of the best benefits of the accountability groups is celebrating everyone's accomplishments and wins. Be a part of a group that wins a lot!

"Connection is why we're here; it's what gives purpose and meaning to our lives.

Dr. Brené Brown

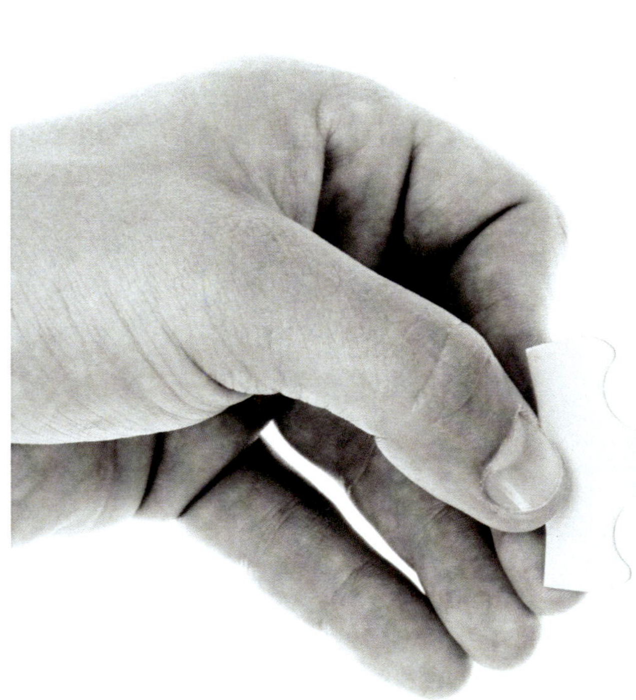

www.sisisityou.com

Characteristics of a Strong Community Member

I have always wondered about my great grandmother's secret to forming her strong community and what characteristics she sought out in her community members. To find answers, you must ask questions. During a conversation with my friend Fran, I complimented her on the strong team she had formed. I was captivated by how they remained loyal and fitting for her. I asked her how she chose such a strong team around her, and her answer was profound. Just a little back story on Fran. She is from Louisiana with an accent that I had just fallen in love with. I will attempt to embody her.

She said, *"BABEEEE, let me tell you I ask the Lord to pick out my friends. I go to God with the approval process and selection process. I pray for discernment, and then I align their values with my core values. If they don't align, they are not my friend."*

As she said this, my mouth dropped because that was my problem. I had never prayed and ask God to reveal to me the people that should be in my life. I figured if we vibed, then that was the connection. I never thought it truly mattered if their core values aligned with mine. As long as they weren't a pedophile, murderer, liar, or thief, it would be clear skies for me.

That was it. I needed to go back and refinance all of my friendships. If you are familiar with a refinance, you get to go back and renegotiate the terms of the contract. If it doesn't go well for you, the refi is canceled. This had to happen.

Member Characteristics to Look For

While reading a book called *The People Factor*, Pastor Moody states that the most valuable person isn't always the most visible person. We go looking for flashy people to be our friends, and often they lack good core values. It is the silent and discreet folks that hold the keys that you need. (Review Chapter 1 on core values to refresh your memory.) To find these people, we have to have good filters to weed out what comes in and what stays out. Look out for these specific characteristics when on this discovery.

Complacency Crushers- People that won't allow you to become complacent in your purpose. These people need to motivate you to aspire to get off your butt and hold you accountable for your purpose—those who don't allow you to be the same person every day.

Wise Owls- People who embody wisdom and good discernment. The importance of this is that they will impart this into you. When you hang around someone for a while, you can inherit some of the traits that belong to them. Wisdom allows you to have an easier time navigating through life and situations successfully.

Unconditional Lovers- People who can offer unconditional love and acceptance can provide you a safe place to be yourself. When you can live freely, you're not worried about the judgment of others. You know that their correction comes out of love, so you let your mistakes be the antidote to your growth.

Non-competitors- People who stretch you to become better are those who don't compete with your accomplishments. These people become your biggest cheerleaders and are consistent and constant with encouragement. We all know a MR. /MRS. ME TOO.

Time Protectors- People can give you their time and energy when you need it versus when you want it. Boy, this will be a hard one for some of you to grasp, so I'm going to break this down. We all are guilty of becoming *Needy Nancy* when we connect with that one person that "TOTALLY" gets us. GUILTY! (Vol. 2-I will get into that). We must learn to separate a need from a want. When we want something, we get overwhelmed with expectation. Imagine when you always want to talk to someone because they offer most of the time a sense of relief from your current issue. What happens if we overuse it? It experiences wear or tear. In this specific example, the type of wear and tear you will experience depreciates what they offer you. (When we need something, and our need is met, we are relieved) Overusing the members in your community will only weaken your community. It also points out that you might not be applying their teachings to your life if you always need them.

Exposure Team- People who can expose you to more than you have experienced in your current life and open you to new possibilities. It tickles me when people complain about never seeing the world but tell me they visit Hawaii every year. Yes, I understand that they enjoy it, but it's because they aren't courageous enough to venture out to other places. That's why it's essential to have these types of members in your community. They will motivate and inspire you to venture out beyond your comfort zone.

Every new possibility is attached to a risk you were willing to take. – Tiffynee

God's Disciples- People who encourage you to be faithful to God's word. Their faithfulness to God inspires you to develop a deeper personal relationship with Him as well. Don't be distracted by the Bible thumpers that use God's word as a weapon to attack others instead of loving others. If you are experiencing a delay in judgment with someone, use these strategies.

- Pray about it to God.
- Ask a member from your wise counsel.
- Wait for an answer
- Don't rush this process.

Integrity Riders- People who are character-driven with integrity leading the way. These people do not need a constant flow of discipline and correction because they are self-correctors. It takes a lot of discipline to be a self-corrector, and it also takes a massive force of intentionality. Their integrity is so deep that they don't have time to live their lives in malicious ways. When you surround yourself with people who have high standards according to how they live, you are inspired to want to live by their values, and you want to experience their peace.

Hitman Squad- People who will defend you whenever it is necessary. We have all been in a room when another person's name is mention negatively in a conversation. We have all had to uncomfortably watch how no one defends that person's name (even just by the simple moral that they aren't there to speak for themselves.) The right type of people in your life will know you well enough and believe in you so much that they will have no problem defending you when others speak against you. It would help if you didn't have to expect this, and it naturally happens with everyone. It takes a special type of person to commit to being a hitman.

Tomorrow Squad- People who are committed to your future and not your past. Notice how I'm not saying that they don't know about your history, but merely that they are not committed to your past dealings. These types of people are not concerned with what you did yesterday. They aren't satisfied with what you accomplished today, and they are people who are laser-focused on your future. They invest their time in where you are going, not where you have been or where you are today.

Gratitude Givers- People who are committed to living a life of gratitude. Surround yourself with people who are consistently motivating you to be thankful for what you have in all aspects of life. These people see the silver lining in everything, and they know that God's grace makes it all possible.

1. Complacency Crushers
2. Wise Owls
3. Unconditional Lovers
4. Non-competitors
5. Time Protectors
6. Exposure Team
7. God's Disciples
8. Integrity Riders
9. Hitman Squad
10. Tomorrow Squad
11. Gratitude Givers

Building your Strong community

NAME: TIFFYNEE
SPECIALTIES: 1-11

The REFINANCE

When you hear the word refinance, you might think of when people refinance loans for their homes, cars or anything that involves a loan. The reason people opt in for a refi is because of the benefits that come with it. It lowers your monthly payment, reduces your interest rate, changes your loan type, can boost your savings and consolidate your debt. When you apply to refinance your loan, a few things are used to determine if you qualify for the refi. Your credit history is one of the most significant areas that is evaluated during this process. The things that can hold you back from getting this refi approved is weak credit, late payments, and collections. The way the Refinace is set up in the economic world really aligns with other aspects of our lives as well. The type of Refi I'm referring to is similar to what banks use. Refinancing my friendships was going to take looking over some specific things before deciding to move forward with the relationship.

Tiff Refinance – trading in your old friendship/relationship for a new one. Creating new friendship terms.

A refinance can be denied but its largely based on the requirements not being met. When creating your Refinance for whomever is going through the process, you must know what things are important to look for. It's like I was determined to do refinances and it was my duty to get trained by the best.

The time had come, and it wasn't going to pretty for me. The most important relationship I needed to do this with, besides my husband, was my best friend Rhondolyn of 1000 years. Before this conversation could happen, I was instructed by the HS (Holy Spirit) to reach out to one of my late great grandmothers' best friends. This particular conversation was a prerequisite for what God was about to do to my relationship with Rhondolyn.

During my intimate, yet, emotional conversation with Mother Rogers, I asked important questions that mattered to my value of friendship. Mother Rogers had been without her bestie since 2011. You see, when your BFF passes away, you're able to identify all the coulda, shoulda, and woulda's you possibly could think of. That day, my grandmothers' BFF gave me so many golden nuggets I could barely carry them all back in my memory.

I have always wondered why it takes so long when people go through a refinance process. It makes sense because there are a lot of things that need to be reviewed.

Shortly after that, it was time to meet with my BFF. When I tell you that this was one of the most challenging moments of my life. I'm not lying. As we began to talk, we got caught up in a brief moment of confusion. We both were trying to understand each other and what we both needed. The spirit of confusion was circling like a vulture. During this moment, I had entertained the thought that maybe this wasn't something we are going to get through. I had the feeling you get when you believe that something that you want isn't going to be yours anymore. I was sure that after evaluating our friendship history we were in desperate need to decide what we really wanted out of the Refinance.

I remember the Spirit speaking to me calmly as we sat on my porch, and tears filled both our eyes. It said to be still, just listen. This is her experience with you, and it is your job to change it. At that moment, I remember asking her a few questions.

1. Did she trust me? Her answer was, *"Yes."*
2. Did she trust me to guide us away from this place right now? Her answer was, *"I believe so."*
3. Where did she see us five years from now? She said, *"Vacationing somewhere fun."* (That was confirmation #1 that I needed. She had let me know there was a future for us.)
4. What do you need from me? I explained that I would no longer be giving her what I thought she needed because I guessed and wasn't guessing right. She said that I needed to be patient and fully understand her.
5. Would you be better with letting me know what you need from me so that I could give you exactly that? She said, *"OK."*

Then I apologized for all that I had done and any ill feelings I had caused over our friendship years. You see, as best friends, we had never really fallen out, but I was aware of times that I had become overbearing, needy, and probably unpleasant to be around. The list of characteristics that I gave you above. She embodies all of those. She is the Mother Rogers to my Ruby Irons, and for that, I will always be willing to adjust to becoming a better person. Our refinance wasn't about what I could get out of the deal. It was about what she could get from me. I love her with my whole heart, and I realized that God was preparing our friendship to go through a more significant storm. About one month later, my BFF lost her father to CHF, the exact thing that was holding my life in the balance. What I have watched my BFF endure has not only shown me admiration for humility, but it has given me great honor to call her a member of my strong community. When the storm came, the hard conversation we had to have about our friendship, I made up in my mind, early on, that this wasn't someone I was willing to let go of just because of my ego and pride.

These types of relationships do not typically form at random. They are something that you should prepare yourself for in the meantime. As said before, lack of preparation for the future keeps you chained to the past. Part of preparing for your future includes identifying the people who will help you get to God's purpose for your life and will support you when you reach it. Ruby Lee Irons embodied every one of these characteristics. As I'm saying this to you, it inspired me to emulate her and require the same things in my members. I hope this chapter inspires others to look for these qualities in your community. I want to point out that you should also incorporate these characteristics and qualities into your daily life. The law of attraction: you attract what you are. It is vital to remove all of the people from your once struggling community and require that all members pass this new screening requirement. There's a difference between haters and people that see clearly. Know the difference and spot them early, but don't be afraid to better yourself based on someone's suggestion to improve you.

Refinance

Tiff Refinance – trading in your old friendship/relationship for a new one. Creating new friendship terms.

What is the cost of the emotional currency you spend in this relationship?

Current Interest Rate

What type of things have you experienced in this relationship Good, Bad, and Ugly that currently stand out to you?

Credit History

Have you let the bad things go?

Forgiveness

What do you see for your relationship in the future?

Credit Score

After Further Review does this relationship deserve to refinanced? Or is this something that you need to let go?

Approved or Not Approved

GOD'S PROMISE

Strong Community
Two are better than one,
because they have a good return for their labor:
If either of them falls down,
one can help the other up.
But pity anyone who falls
and has no one to help them up.
Also, if two lie down together, they will keep
warm.
But how can one keep warm alone?
Though one may be overpowered,
two can defend themselves.
A cord of three strands is not quickly broken.

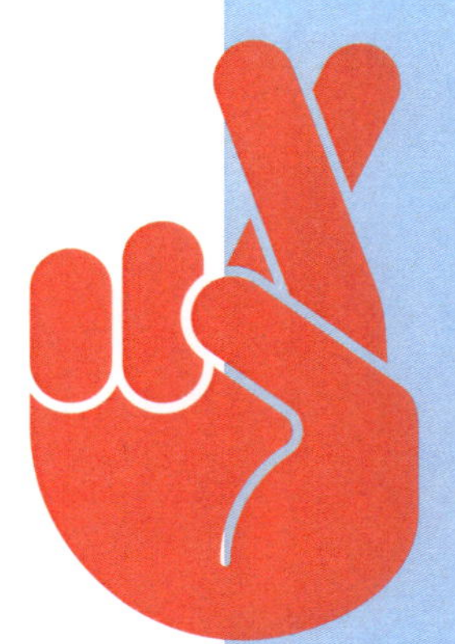

Ecclesiastes 4:9-12 Niv

THE TIFFANATOR

Talk to God

This is one of the easiest things to do because it's just like journaling but with a purpose and person in mind.

CHAPTER 7

THE BAG - BE ACCOUNTABLE

The bag

I t's time to gather all your belongings and pack them up in your bag.

*"**Ninety-nine percent** of all **failures** come from people who have a habit of making excuses."*

- George Washington Carver.

Merriam-Webster's dictionary definition of accountability is: The quality or state of being accountable, *especially* an obligation or willingness to accept responsibility or to account for one's actions.

Accepting accountability can sound easy, but most people struggle with it. They have difficulties realizing that there are discrepancies between their actions and words. People must acknowledge the severe warning signs when becoming aware of this. Once you start digging the hole of avoiding accountability, it is a struggle to dig yourself back out. When pointing out what accountability is, people tend to steer away from the meaning of the word. They disassociate taking account of their actions from taking account of what happened. Do you see what I just did there? When I ask you to take accountability, I'm not referring to what anyone else did. Take account of all your actions, and do not compare to anyone. My expectation is for you to align yourself with the definition and to act upon it.

What do I mean by "taking accountability?"

I once helped a client construct a letter to make the first steps in reconciliation of a relationship she was wanting to salvage. This letter was the first step to her taking accountability and encouraging healing in their relationship. The client had been struggling with this relationship for years and after listening to her I realized she lacked the ability to take accountability for most of her actions. The client acknowledged that everything in the letter was true but wasn't fully ready to give her partner access to that side of her yet. If I'm honest, it was too much for them to receive and accept, and they politely declined to use the letter in their reconciliation. Here's how the letter went.

"Dear My Love,

I finally caught up with my coach and had a session to talk about you and I. I wanted to gain some clarity and get an outside view on our current issue. I started from where I thought things took a turn for the worst, which was when I sent you the email with a breakdown of our problem. She allowed me to finish my story, and then she let me have it. She called me out on all my shit. To be honest, I wanted to hurry and get off the phone because, usually, that isn't the shit I want to hear. She didn't even give me a chance to do so, so I had to sit there and take it. Hell, I paid for it! You know, many of my friends don't stand up to me because I will immediately cut them off. Coach doesn't care if I don't talk to her, lol, which doesn't surprise me much. I honor her for staying faithful to the truth and not just trying to retain a client.

She allowed me to see things from her perspective and correlating my viewpoint. I honestly can say that I didn't know and never took into account how things would leave you feeling after an argument or disagreement. She called me petty and told me that I was wrong for adding the miscellaneous stuff to prove that I do a lot for you. She asked me why I was doing those things for you and I replied with because I love you and genuinely love helping others. She stated it wasn't about what I was doing for you, but she showed me how to separate my good deeds from how you make me feel which was unappreciated.

I'm open to expressing my thoughts and the details of situations between us, but I fail to express my feelings majority of the time. I sat back and started thinking about how I fail to validate your feelings and experiences as well. It never dawned on me that there was a difference in getting things off my chest for my benefit versus censoring my words when trying to get you to understand how I feel about something. Coach pointed out that my objective when communicating with you is for you to understand what I'm saying and that has a lot to do with my delivery method.

Everything she was saying started to hit me like a ton of bricks. I felt offended at first because I thought to myself, that is not who I am or what I'm about. This whole time I had been trying to prove to you that I was about family (something that I cherish and wish I had). It didn't dawn

Dear Jane or John Doe

Write a letter to someone that you need or want to be accountable to ..

on me that I might have come across money hungry or anxious for the next come up. Coach showed me that there is a huge difference from my reality versus what your actual experience is. My intentions didn't reflect my actions or my words, and for that, I genuinely apologize. I have failed to realize that I'm the creator of my drama in my life. Being the creator, I need to learn the correct way of handling things. I have done it my way for years and rarely try out other people's way. If the results don't come quickly, I go back to my inefficient way of thinking. This behavior has ultimately been my demise. I say things out of anger and act irrationally when things are not going according to my plan or expectations. This letter isn't a cop-out. I am trying to become aware of my ish and get a grasp of my life and change things. Coach explained that even though we had an agreement, you are not obligated to do anything outside of our original agreement. I was not too fond of that part. I felt a sense of entitlement because I thought I had earned my piece of the pie over the years because of all the shit I have had to endure over the years with you. She reminded me that I needed to take accountability for all of my actions and not partially. She reminded me that I couldn't just pick and choose what I'm responsible for because it didn't sound good to me. This process is just the beginning of me trying to change and stick to it, and it won't happen overnight. It takes consistency and determination for me to be a better me and stop trying to blame you for all my downfalls.

Sincerely,

Jane Doe"

Accountability takes vulnerability, courage, humility, intentionality, strong community and knowing where your heart really is. This isn't something easy but it's worth it.

Accountability Starts with You

To create a culture of accountability, it starts with you. You need to model the behaviors that you want to see gravitating towards you. The law of attraction means you attract what you are. Take ownership of those things and make commitments. You must meet those commitments. If you don't, then why should anyone else be interested in doing so? My husband and my youngest are quite similar in their ability to avoid accountability. We are currently working on some solutions.

Every day, I walk into my bedroom and see many belongings that do not belong to me on my coffee table. I take inventory of who those things belong to and how they got into my room. Once I have completed my scan, I do what most parents would do. I sit down and pretend it isn't mine. Ok, not that time, but it sounded good. I call both my daughters into the room and tell them to grab their things and put them away. My 8-year-old, 79 in spirit, can take account of everything that anyone else does, including herself. Now, don't give her kudos just yet. Her ability to accept responsibility is all dependent on who touches it last. I watch them grab some of their stuff, and I remind my 8-year old that there are a few more things of hers left on the table. She turned to me with a straight face and said, *"That is my stuff, but I didn't touch it last. It isn't my responsibility to put it back where it came from."*

Pick your mouth up off the floor. Yes, she said it, and she meant it. These moments come in handy when you locate the root of the problem. You need to attend to it before it spirals out of control. This problem was spiraling out of control!

Accountability isn't a one-time thing.

Once my husband and I noticed that this was becoming a recurring problem with her, it was time to attack the root. I told my husband that I couldn't be the only one displaying accountability because it was causing an imbalance in our household. It was going to take the both of us to show her how important this characteristic was.

Accountability is not a one-time, sometimes thing. It's an all-time thing. Some people don't want to be held accountable. They are constantly looking for any opportunities to get out of any slip-ups. These people typically use phrases or words like these to give them the out they need to only be accountable when they see fit.

- Mostly
- Kind of
- Sort of
- Not really
- Too a degree
- A bit

Put it in the Bag

Let's take account of the things in your life.
Place all of things that belong to you in this bag!

Most of the time, we will take account of other people's stuff, but rarely our own. Pick up all your ish and place it in this bag!

These are just a few on the top of my list because these are my husband's and kids' favorite go-to's when they are trying to evade accountability. You always need to be accountable, not just when it is convenient or when the weight of failure is too heavy for you to carry. My husband hates to be wrong but doesn't like to ask for much help. So, the odds are against him when he chooses to guess at everything. He wants to take partial accountability when things come, just as our daughter does. To them, it wasn't ALL their faults. They both settled for either some or none. The three-letter word **ALL** rarely visits their vocabulary.

Accountability is the difference between success and failure.

When people don't take accountability and things start to go wrong, they step into spectator mode and watch as things fail. If you don't feel ownership over something, you see no value in it, and that leads to destruction. I frequently tell my husband that he doesn't allow room for improvement when he fails to take full responsibility for things.

Imagine going to the doctor and saying, *"My foot hurts."*

The doctor asks you how you hurt it, and your reply is, *"I sort of kicked the wall."*

Right there, at that moment, the doctor is trying to wrap his head around how you sort of did something. Either you kicked the wall purposely, accidentally bumped into the wall with your leg (I know that sounds crazy), or you didn't kick the wall at all. The person is only using the words "sort of" because it remits some guilt of actually kicking the wall and being hurt.

When things start to go wrong, and the person takes ownership, then they step into solution mode. They begin to figure out what's going wrong and try and fix it. When something happens to me, my first thought is to own up to what I did or go straight into a solution focused mindset. There is a vast difference in my hubby's failures and successes versus mine. The single biggest differentiator between being successful and unsuccessful is being purposeful in the ability to take accountability.

Accountability up close

- People recognize and own up to their part of what is occurring.
- If their message is hurtful to someone, they are willing to examine how their communication may have been unhealthy or damaging.
- They don't blame others when they are at fault.
- They don't make excuses for why things are happening.

- They don't pawn off all the failure onto others close to them.
- If their relationships are faltering, they are open to seeing how they contribute to the challenges and conflict.
- They can see and understand the other person's perspective even if they disagree.
- They recognize that what is happening in their world and how their accountability actively shapes their beliefs and actions.

Here are some ways to become more accountable for yourself, your actions, and your words today.

- **Recognize how are you contributing to this problem.**

  Yes, this is part of being accountable. What is your contribution? Don't be modest and just acknowledge the fact that you are present during the problem. Dig deep within yourself. I'm sure that there are a few things that belong to you.

  If I could credit anyone who helped my marriage, it would be my best friend, Tosha. I would intentionally go to her when my husband and I would be at odds because I knew she would always point out how I was contributing to the problem.

- Tone
- Assumptions
- Inability to receive criticism
- (many other things. Take your pick, don't worry, we will wait!)

- **Discover where you feel most hurt in life and get help to heal.**

  Do you know how much of our past has to do with the everyday things we get offended by? What is not transformed is transferred into your daily life. You have to recognize that it may not be your fault, but it is your responsibility to deal with it. The odds of you becoming what you hate because you never allowed yourself to heal are pretty high when you ignore your past. Forgive and let go!

- **Apologize make it a *real* apology.**

  The next time you do something wrong, apologize. This apology isn't just an "I'm sorry"— make it a genuine apology.

- **Acknowledge that you're toxic to others.**

  SIS/BRO. This is big and what the next volume is all about! We tend to drop toxic turds around us and refuse to bring a poop bag to pick it up. It's equivalent to when someone farts, and no one wants to own up to it. Yes, you stink! It's time to recognize that you're toxic and identifying what that looks like is the most challenging task of them all.

Maintain your Integrity

The book called *People Factor* by Pastor Moody talks about the four ingredients to integrity. He states that the best way to know if someone has integrity is to observe them during a crisis. When a person is in a situation where conflict and pressure arise, a person's character is challenged and spotlighted.

Your commitment to the truth.
The truth must be the foundation of any relationship but, most importantly, the one you have with yourself. When you're strong and mature, you're not willing to compromise the truth. These types of people dare to deal with the consequences of their reality. You must know that trust is built in tiny moments. Anything can be rebuilt with the truth.

Refusal to compromise your core values.
Whenever a person compromises their integrity, they ultimately lose what they were trying to hold on to. Yes, they might experience a brief moment of instant gratification, but it will soon dissipate. This just doesn't affect you, it affects the people around you.

Dedication to your motives.
Your motives should always align with your core values. There is wanting to do right and doing right. They both need to coexist. Assessing your motives requires you to ask yourself some honest questions, and you must be honest with yourself. Being a person who has impure motives can ruin your life, so make sure your heart's posture is right!

Consistent pursuit of excellence.
Excellence demands a constant and consistent effort. You must become passionate about achieving excellence, not perfection. This requires time and energy. You cannot accomplish

this alone, so it is essential to have a strong community behind you. It is much easier when you are not alone during this pursuit.

You have to hold people accountable.

You can't just tell people they're accountable and then leave them to take ownership of it. Yes, it may work for some people, but not for all. Consistency is necessary when applying this to your life.

What I see with my eyes, I also see with your actions.

"I'm not a thief or a liar," she repeatedly said to me, her mother.

I scolded her for about two solid minutes. *"Jai, where is my bronzer!"*

"Mom, I swear I don't have it," she said quietly over the phone. *"Mom, I wouldn't take your bronzer, especially after you told me last time to not touch your stuff!"* she said proudly.

"Jai, you are a thief and a liar. Do you honestly think that I believe a word you said?" I sarcastically replied.

"Mom, I'm not a liar and definitely not a thief. Why would you say something like that!" she cried.

As she heard the words liar and thief come out my mouth, she immediately went into full acting mode. She became defensive and then proceeded to act like how dare I call her liar and a thief! Even though we all know that I have a 13-year-old daughter in that exploratory stage of makeup, we know who had the bronzer. She returned it about two days later. She, then, acted like I wouldn't notice that it was back in my makeup bag (that's clear). When I saw it was back in the bag, I went to her and sat her down.

I said, *"You lied to me again and stole from me which makes you a thief."*

As the *"ffff"* left my mouth, her tears started flowing like waterworks. Suppose you don't like being associated with the words that I call you. It is totally within your control to remove the actions that define the comments. The stories will eventually disappear from her record. I grabbed her hand and said, *"If you tell me you didn't take something, but you did indeed take it, what did you do?"*

She replied, *"I lied."*

I said, *"I asked you several times and what did you do?"*

She said, *"I lied."*

I said, *"What would you call yourself, a truthteller?"*

She said, *"I guess a liar."*

This story just exhibits that if one of your members of your strong community points something out and it's a consistent thing, instead of taking on an offense, let's take a step back and think why this person would say this or what you have done to create that type of speculation.

Lets Think About It 

To the faithful, you show yourself faithful; to those with integrity you show integrity.
(2 Samuel 22:26, NLT)

Doing the right thing when no one is watching . What does integrity look like for you ?

What is integrity?

Who do you know that has integrity?

Are honesty and integrity the same thing?

What do they do that is kind?

What does it mean to be kind?

GOD'S PROMISE

Accountability
So, whoever knows the right
thing to do and fails to do it, for
him it is sin.

James 4:17 ESV

THE TIFFANATOR

Talk to God

This is one of the easiest things to do because it's just like journaling but with a purpose and person in mind.

What's in your Bag?

Let's take inventory of the things that we have gathered throughout this book. Check off the items you understand and go back and study the things that you didn't quite grasp. Don't be in a rush to get all of these in one read, and they take time to develop. That means don't go letting your ego and pride check all these boxes prematurely. Have integrity and humility while doing this simple activity.

A Map

Metal Detector

Pin Pointer

Shovel

Sifter

Bag

Table

CHAPTER 8

TABLE - REFLECTIONS

The table is for you to use when you collect all your unique findings. You will spread them out on the table to get a good look at what you need to work on. This table will allow you to spread things out, separate, sort, and prioritize what you first want to start working on as you make your way through this discovery.

What's in your bag?

Welcome! I wasn't sure if you were going to make it to the end because I struggled to get to this point myself. During this journey, I expected a swiper to pop up and throw a wrench in our plan. It's why I left trails of God's promises throughout the book so. Like Hansel and Gretel, you too would find your way to the end. Now that we have a backpack full of useful tools, I'll fill you in on how we plan on using each one through the next phase of our discovery. SIS, is it you realizing the toxic you?

The Map

As we dive into this next book, the map will allow us to see a glimpse of ourselves in others' stories. It will alert us that something is triggering a conviction in our spirit, and we must have good intentions not to ignore it but to bring out the next set of tools to help identify the real issue. This revelation isn't just going to happen once or twice. This will be an ongoing tool that you use in life moving forward. Your toxic meter will alert you when you have buried a toxin instead of disposing of it as you should. We can't avoid certain toxins that happen to get into our bodies. Once we become aware of it, it is our job to escort it out politely, or forcefully whatever tends to work better for you.

The Metal Detector- Intentionality

The Metal Detector will help us precisely locate where the toxin is. When we become intentional about who we are supposed to be, it is easy to pinpoint the things that don't belong. Just think about when we all use to play that game on Sesame Street. One of the items looks like the other, and one of these things doesn't belong. Become familiar with the things that stand out in your life. It will also help contribute to you picking your strong community and taking accountability. This tool is multifaced because it isn't just good for one thing. It serves many purposes. When I became intentional about what was for me and what wasn't, my life took a dramatic turn for the better. This doesn't mean life is easy. This means that I have made it easier by creating a plan and being intentional. I also had to become intentional with being healthy. I have the heart to protect!

The Metal Probe-Humility

You are getting a taste of what type of soil you're digging up using the metal probe. The metal probe will help keep you stable through this next process. Having the ability to encompass humility while trying to uncover your toxins will be essential. Your toxins will cause you to clam up because it is hard to point out things with reasoning and logic attached to them. Humility will allow you to be okay with areas in your life that might not look all bright and shiny up close.

You will get to say, *"I'm human. I'm flawed. I mess up, and I will change."*

Once we start uncovering or noticing the toxic turds you have left a trail of, it's your responsibility to get a doggy bag, pick your shit up and dispose of it. We are trying to avoid people stepping in it to leave it on the ground exposed. My friend Candice Kelley once said, while we were on Instagram Live, that she was the expert on knowing herself and that she was so aware of who she was that she didn't allow others to persuade her from knowing otherwise.

The Shovel/Digger- Courage

While working on ourselves, we have to dig up many things buried deep within us. The shovel represents the audacity prevalent in your life right now. This shovel will give us the courage to keep digging until we get what we are looking for. We didn't come this far only to give up. You're going to need the courage to face the things that were sent to destroy the inner you. You're going to need to deconstruct the walls of fear to get to peace and happiness.

You must have the nerve to say, *"TOXINS, you once resided here, but no more."*

Remember, there will be times when those arms will get tired of digging, and they will ache. That is when you take a brief break and reach out to your strong community. You were sent here with a mission, and the one thing that is going to stop you is your lack of strength. My courage has been driven because of my desire to grow, and I have learned, and now understand, that to be inevitable. So, you will have to go through Grown Painz.

(Shameless plug, but a real-life journey.) My husband and I have endured and grown so much together. It takes courage to keep your relationship going. You might be thinking, why do I have to be courageous to be in a relationship? Think of all the times you wanted to give up because you thought things wouldn't change. It takes courage, faith, and strength to continue striving for something if you can see the end goal. Shout out to #Relationshipgoals Pastor Mike Todd and his beautiful wife Natalie. They have also displayed their growing pains, but the Big Homie GOD keeps His promises.

Dirt Sifter-Strong Community

The dirt sifter helps to remove the toxins in your life. Your strong community is the company you keep. The dirt sifter makes sure you sift out all the things that don't belong. It has many tiny holes that make sure the things that belong go back into your soil and the big things that don't belong are sorted through and taken out. Your group members will be impactful during this stage of your discovery. I say this because you will try and reason why something can stay, and you will need someone that you trust to ask you important questions to help you realign yourself with God purpose for your life. It will be someone from your community who will possess the type of discernment to shut down that belief of yours and counter it with logic. Don't allow the cognitive dissonance to interfere with your ability to grow and get rid of the baggage you do not need. Side note: if your homegirls aren't reading this book, they have to go! Everyone in your strong community needs the same fruit as you. Feed your spirit and theirs! www.SisIsItYou.com

The Bag- Accountability

 Who doesn't want to know what's in the bag? I sure don't. Not this particular bag. This bag needs to be sorted through and disposed of, but before you can do that, you have to make sure that you deal with the things in the bag. The contents in the bag aren't pretty. They are unfamiliar but they belong to you. This bag reeks! Guess what? It's your stuff. Sis, it's you! What we get to do with this bag comes in book three. We get to put all these things on the table and deal with them one by one. We know that they belong to us, but we aren't giving them to a new owner. We are getting rid of them forever. Who would want to pass this crap on? You know the saying, *"I wouldn't wish that on my worst enemy?"* Stick with that. This bag is only here to teach us, help us grow, and move on to the next challenge. This is not something that you drop off at the Good Will. Even they don't want this junk. I hate garbage, and most of my toxins are straight funky garbage, and if you are like me, that crap makes you nauseous. I have found a way to turn myself into a garbage disposal. I state whatever it is about me that I know isn't good for me around someone I know will start to inquire about it. They then ask logical questions that my Sane Self knows don't align with my morals, values, and principles. For example, I can't tell my kids to watch their mouths when my mouth is foul. Triggered? That just triggered me. Wooo weee that convicted me. If your children see you always cussing someone out or talking to people crazy, please be aware that they will be doing the same thing or will attract the same thing. Be the best mirror you can. When you make mistakes own up to them. When you offend someone, apologize, or ask if you have offended them. Check the intent of your heart at all times. Most of you reading this book won't believe that I practice what I preach because I don't. That daughter of mine, Jordyn, comes for my neck. It's equivalent to your grandparents checking you. Be mindful of what you're putting out to the world and if it happens to be a mistake, own up to it, correct it and be better next time.

Many of you have a problem with the Bible because you think it has too many rules and regulations. I hate to break it to you, but these are the same principles you live by. You don't want to attach them to the Big Homie God because you don't like anyone telling you what to do. Isn't it silly to follow rules but say that you won't give someone recognition because you want the credit? Remember to be humble.

For the record, your parents are your parents. You don't get to pick them. So, God is God, and He made them parents of yours.

The Table-Reflections

Now we are here. Everything is out on the table, so let's take a look. The next few worksheets will walk you through this phase. Until next time, I'll see you soon. Hopefully, you have signed up for the self-revelation challenge on www.friskyfemme.com/challenges.

Sis, is it you? Realizing the Toxic in you is where we will see a depiction of the things that we do that are toxic. We have come to realize that not all toxins are bad otherwise, we would be nonexistent. It is the number of toxins in your body. Too much of anything only leaves you contaminated. If you are contaminated, you will not function correctly. Covid 19 has taught us this: some of us survived it, and some of our bodies couldn't take the contamination (Rest in Peace to all those who have lost their lives to Covid 19). I have been on the side of contamination, and it has cost me so much, but it has also taught me a lot. I know I get to be a resource and share my story and my tool with the world. So, get ready. We are going to detox! Sis, it was me, and it is you. But Sis, let's do this together.

 Lets Think About It

Just as water mirrors your face, so your face mirrors your heart.
Proverbs 27:19

Ask yourself these questions

How is my progress looking compared to my last evaluation?

Is this what God wants for my life?

What have I accomplished lately?

What things have held me back this year?

What are some of the critical learning moments I had this year?

GOD'S PROMISE

Reflection

To the Jews who had believed him, Jesus said, "If you hold to my teaching, you are really my disciples. Then you will know the truth, and the truth will set you free.".

John 8:31-32 Niv

Talk to God

This is one of the easiest things to do because it's just like journaling but with a purpose and person in mind.

____
____
____
____
____
____
____
____
____
____
____
____
____
____
____
____
____
____
____
____
____

THE TIFFANATOR

It's me, Tiffynee, your accountability partner.
Let's reflect on all the things we have gathered and place them on the table to get a good look at everything!
These tools are designed to help you work towards achieving a better life.

RUBY'S PRECIOUS GEM

Hello Everyone,
This is the day that the Lord has made, and I will rejoice and be glad in it.
Amen!
My great-granddaughter Tiffynee has taken a gift I gifted her long ago and put it down on paper. Now do me a favor because you know I don't ask for much and scan this QR code below and check out the
Sis, is it you?
Discovering Self Revelation devotional.

Acknowledgements

The reason I smile is that God is so good to me. I want first to acknowledge that throughout this entire process, God has been right beside me and in me. I'm humbled, honored, and happy that I got to put this on paper and that you are getting to read it, so THANK YOU. Finally, I want to take the time out to acknowledge my family, team, friends, and my community.

To my fine as wine husband, and so much more **Brandon Q. Thomas-** Your love for me is a pure gift from God, and I'm so thankful that he chose for us to be together. Thank you for never giving up on me and never letting me go even though I was a runner and a track star. Thank you for showing me so much grace and mercy through my toxic and detoxing phases. Your prayers and love for me allowed me to grow into the woman I am today. Thank you for being an amazing father to our girls, Jai and Jordyn. They bring purpose to my life and revelation, BRO it was me...lol. You will be my forever partner, my heart, and my love.

To my parents, JT $, and My wonderful mother, Sheila A.T.P (lol), I want to thank you for doing the nasty and giving me a chance to grace this earth. Your parenting styles have shaped me into the person I am today. I thank you both for always being willing to recognize Tiff, and it is you …lol. Thank you for allowing Ruby Lee Irons to play such an instrumental part in my life. I know back then I didn't understand why, but the *WHO* was so much bigger than the WHY! It took me a long time to grasp that, but I thank you both for everything. My humor, wit, tenacity, ability to dream, and honestly, the space big enough for me to be me. I love you both dearly. Thank you!

To My Besties and My Riders- You all were awesome throughout this process, and all played significant positions in this coming to pass.

Andrene- Thank you for pushing me to make this book phenomenal. You challenged me every step of the way to come harder and to bring it. Thank you for allowing me to learn from you and being open with me because that helped me grow!

Tariana- Neicy poo, you are terrific from head to toe, and I can't wait to see what you bring to this world. I want to thank you for doing all the first round of editing for me and encouraging me to clear up my thoughts and expand on my thinking. You are a true gem.

Rhondolyn-Thank you for all the tiny little details you went over at the crack of dawn and at the last minute. You were just there always and forever for me. Thank you for refinancing us and giving me an excellent interest rate.

Tosha-You are the GOAT. If I could put into words what you were doing for me, we both might be attacked by tree huggers. Thank you for being there, always and forever, for me.

Tangie- From the moment you were born, I knew we would be inseparable, makes sense why we bumped heads so much. Your patience and support for me has been the most encouraging thing ever. You make me feel loved like no other. If your love and support for me is anything identical to how Grandma Linda would have, I'm a fortunate person. Thank you so much for being you.

Akea-The push and the idea were birthed from you, and then the motivation to make it to a book was just the Holy Spirit speaking through you to me. Thank you for everything that you have done for me throughout this process. You are one of a kind, and I'm thankful for your friendship and helpful guidance.

Andrea- To the wise owl: Your wisdom and the rekindling of our friendship has allowed me to expand my conversation and ideas to a greater level. Thank you for being you! I love you always and forever.

Shontee- Big Sissy, alert, thank you for helping me always sort my thoughts and push me forward to my next task. You are much needed. I love you dearly.

My SEXOLOGIST BESTIES
Nikkita Steven Cecelia

All three of you came at different seasons of this process, but neither of you have left me yet. Your support for me and the fact that I have never seen either one of you face to face is unreal. I'm truly blessed to call you guys my family. I can't wait to work with all of you, but as of right now, I want to thank you for helping me get to this point. I love you all dearly.

My Rich in spirit Besties